SOME OF THE LOS[ING GAMES] THAT MEN PLAY

—The Macho Warrior with The Earth Mother
 (until she brings him down with a thud)

—The Stiff Upper Lip When In Pain
 (the next step is rigor mortis)

—The One Who Never Fails
 (even at suicide)

—The Decision Maker for Both Him and Her
 (and the one who takes all the blame)

—The Stud
 (getting it up until you collapse)

—The Bringer Home of the Bacon
 (even when no one is hungry)

Now there is a groundbreaking new book that tells the endangered male sex how to save themselves from these and other destructive stereotypes—

THE NEW MALE
From Self-Destruction to Self-Care

"Dr. Herb Goldberg's *The Hazards of Being Male* has become the bible of the men's movement . . . *The New Male* is a worthy successor!"—THE AMERICAN MAN Magazine

"Challenging and needed!"—HOUSTON CHRONICLE

SIGNET and MENTOR Books of Interest

THE NEW MALE

From Self-Destruction to Self-Care

by
Herb Goldberg

Ⓢ
A SIGNET BOOK
NEW AMERICAN LIBRARY
TIMES MIRROR

Grateful acknowledgment is made for permission to quote from the following:
"The Hill Wife," from *The Poetry of Robert Frost* edited by Edward Connery Lathem. Copyright 1916, © 1969 by Holt, Rinehart and Winston. Copyright 1944 by Robert Frost. Reprinted by permission of Holt, Rinehart and Winston, Publishers.
"About a Man" by Mark Strand. From *The Late Hour* (Atheneum). Reprinted by permission; © 1977 The New Yorker Magazine, Inc.

Copyright © 1979 by Herb Goldberg

First Signet Printing, August, 1980

1 2 3 4 5 6 7 8 9

PRINTED IN THE UNITED STATES OF AMERICA

For my mother, Ella,
My sisters, Paula Nelson and
Bernice Wiesel, and their families,
My dear buddies George Bach and Marx Ayres,
And to the women who have been in my life
and who have given me my highest, most
euphoric moments and my lowest, most despairing
ones—may we someday meet happily on the
middle ground.

Acknowledgments

The "magical" part of writing a book is the people who appear during its development and either directly or indirectly make an important contribution. Without them a project such as this one would be significantly diminished.

Foremost, I would like to acknowledge with warm appreciation Ms. Nicole Howell, whose careful and faithful assistance in compiling research material as well as attending to the references and footnoting of this book were a source of great help and comfort. In addition, my thanks go to Ms. Rita Elwell, Ms. Donna Anderson and Ms. Beverly Britt for providing case studies, Mr. Earl Goldman for his contribution in the area of statistics on childhood emotional disorders, and Ms. Renae Jones for her fine work in typing the manuscript.

Finally, my editors, James Landis and Maria Guarnaschelli, who bolstered my work with their sensitivity, skills and support, and Mr. Francis Greenburger for his excellent work in finding a suitable home for this book.

HERB GOLDBERG

May, 1979

Contents

Introduction

In recent years there has been a dramatic change in the perception and functioning of the male in our culture. It has become increasingly apparent that the gender orientation known as masculinity has serious and troubling limitations and, consequently, has put the male clearly in crisis. He is accused of being chauvinistic and oppressive. He is fearful of abandonment by his increasingly autonomous and powerful woman. He is burning himself out physically and emotionally in pursuit of a success trip and other goals whose fruits are all too often questionable and meager. He hears and reads endless discussions about his declining sexual performance and increasing "dysfunction" supposedly caused by women's new assertiveness. He is lacking a support system with other men to help him through these crises, and he possesses little insight into the causes of what is happening to him and has few inner resources to draw on for nourishment during the difficult periods. He is truly a cardboard goliath, unable to flow self-caringly with the changing social scene.

Every crisis, however, provides fruitful soil for growth in addition to potential for disaster. Positive change and growth are more possible now than ever before. The social revolutions of recent years can lessen the male's time-honored burdens, help him reclaim denied emotion, expand his sensual responsiveness, bring new dimensions of honesty and depth of his heterosexual relationships, as well as alert him to the self-destructive compulsions within him.

It was my purpose in writing this book to explore how things have traditionally been for the male, and between him and her; how they are in today's era of changing women's consciousness, and how they might someday become as he begins to examine, reshape and expand his own role behavior and self-awareness.

Exploring the roots and implications of gender conditioning is, for me, the most exciting frontier in the field of psychology today. Through this book, I hope to contribute to a new understanding and recasting of the postures of masculinity in the direction of self-care, totalness and a feeling process that would facilitate the kinds of transparency, fluidity and fulfillment that the traditional masculine harness has previously made it near impossible for him to achieve.

HERB GOLDBERG

May 1979

PART ONE

HE

1. The Cardboard Goliath

ABOUT A MAN

Would get up at night,
go to the mirror and ask:
Who's here?

Would turn, sink to his knees
and stare at snow falling blameless
in the night air.

Would cry:
Heaven, look down!
See? No one is here.

Would take off his clothes and say:
My flesh is a grave with nothing inside.

Would lean to the mirror:
You there, you, wake me,
tell me none of what I've said is true.
                    —Mark Strand[1]

Women bend and men break. The blueprint for masculinity is a blueprint for self-destruction. It is a process so deeply embedded in the male consciousness, however, that awareness of its course and its end has been lost. The masculine imperative, the pressure and compulsion to perform, to prove himself, to dominate, to live up to the "masculine ideal"—in short, to "be a man"—supersedes the instinct to survive. His psychological fragility and volatility may even cause him to destroy a lifetime of work and relationships in a momentary impulse.

The diagnosis of chauvinism is superficial. More often it is a gross and misleading distortion. Closer examination of a man's behavior reveals a powerfully masochistic, self-hating and often pathetically self-destructive style.

The brittle male conducts his life by his *ideas* about masculinity. Living up to the *image* is the important thing. Though the moment-to-moment experience may be painful and generally unsatisfying for him, his mind is continually telling him *what he is supposed to be*. As long as he is able to be that way, he can fend off the inner demons that threaten him with accusations of not being "a man."

As his isolation and distrust, the hallmarks of "successful" masculinity, increase, so do his drive for power and control and his inner rage and frustration. He senses the human experience drifting beyond his reach forever. By trying to control the world, even "improve" it or change it, he may simply be trying to make it a place in which he can safely become human—more loving and less aggressive. But the plan fails. His great hunger to prove himself, plus his anger and distrust, drive the possibilities of intimacy away. As his life unfolds and he is well into living up to masculine expectations, his behavior and choices for emotional nourishment may very well become more desperate and bizarre.

Traditional masculinity is largely a psychologically defensive operation rather than an authentic and organic process. A man's psychological energy is used to defend *against*, rather than to express, what he really is. His efforts are directed at proving to himself and others what *he is not*: feminine, dependent, emotional, passive, afraid, helpless, a loser, a failure, impotent and so on. He burns himself out in this never-ending need to prove, because he can *never* sufficiently prove it. To his final day he is driven to project himself as "a man," whether on the battlefield, behind the desk, in lovemaking, on the hospital operating table, in a barroom or even on his deathbed. And when he fails, his self-hate and humiliation overwhelm him.

He would sooner die than acknowledge the things that threaten him most. And yet his deepest imprint is feminine, for it was a woman, not a man, who was his lifeline and his deepest source of identification when he was a baby and a young boy. The femininity is therefore naturally a part of his core. The stronger that identification is and the more it threatens, the more powerfully will he need to deny it. Prisons, as well as violent street gangs, are filled with men who have "Mother" tattooed on their arm, and "motherfucker" as the trigger insult that may well bring death or serious injury to the one who dares to utter it.

In the traditional contemporary American home, the feminine imprint is particularly deep because the father sees himself as an incompetent, bumbling parent whose only legitimate territory is the office or the factory. He defers to the innate "maternal wisdom" of his wife in the early child-rearing process. Or he is by necessity simply minimally present, consumed by economic pressures. He is a father in name rather than in behavior; his role is to keep the bills paid and provide for the necessities of life. In many cases, divorce has made him largely a stranger to his family.

The emotions are there, but the admonitions against expressing them have progressively caused them to be blocked out of consciousness. As a boy the message he received was clear: Feelings are taboo.

Recently I conducted a marathon therapy group for married couples in a small city in the Midwest, where most of the men still behave in gender-traditional ways. I began by asking each man to write about his feelings, about his life as it was for him, and about his marriage. Five of the eight men insisted that they had *no feelings* inside themselves at all. With assistance, they eventually began to get in touch with their emotions, and it was not hard to understand why they had been blocked. Feelings of frustration, resentment, conflict, loneliness and of not being cared for lay underneath. The men were afraid of these emotions and would not know how to deal with them if they acknowledged them. On the surface, in self-protection, all of these men were "macho"—detached, hyperrational and tough—in short, machinelike. Of course, all of them drank before coming home each day after work, and heavily on weekends. They were burning out rapidly in every way.

The feminist movement has brought the man's rigidity forth in maximal relief. If his fear of change weren't so powerful, he would embrace the movement for the life-giving and life-expanding possibilities it offers him: a release from age-old guilt and responsibility toward women and from many onerous burdens. And if he could redefine himself and perceive women differently, he could begin to achieve the rebirth in heterosexual relationships that would come from equal responsibility and comfortable self-expression. However, unable to change, he is afraid of women's changing, too. As a result of his rigidity, the transformation in women only spells danger in the form of abandonment and potential emotional starvation.

It is my interpretation that on the deepest archetypal level the feminist movement is partially fueled by an intuitive sensing of the decay and demise of the male. Women are rushing in to take men's places, as much for survival's sake as for any sociological or philosophical reasons. He has become a hyperactive, hyper-cerebral, hyper-mechanical, rigid, self-destructive machine out of control.

In 1910 there were 106.2 men for every 100 women in the population at large. By 1970, about the time when the feminist movement began to develop momentum, there were approximately 94.8 men for every 100 women.[2] In 1978, by age sixty-five, there were only 75 men left for every 100 women. Little boys fall prey to major illnesses, such as hyperkinesis, autism, stuttering and so on, at rates several hundred percent higher than little girls. The suicide rate for men is also several times higher than for women, to say nothing of the many indirect and less obvious ways in which men kill themselves. And the behavior of the up-and-coming generations of men suggests that the self-destructive trend may be accelerating.

In an article entitled "My Lost Generation," the author describes the men he grew up with in the 1960s in this way: "When I speak of my lost generation, I mean mainly the men. I am told by veteran editors that, by as early as 1965, more good women and fewer good men began passing through their offices, getting assignments and eventually becoming writers. . . . There has been a change, a shift. In the sixties, we used to sing a song that now seems a little too sentimental: 'Where have all the young men gone . . . ?' It is still a good question. Many of my friends have gone to graveyards, real and otherwise."[3]

The nature of masculinity is such that the male is unable even to recognize that he is in hazard. His life seems to him to be totally within his control. Unaccustomed to self-examination, he blocks out awareness of the way he lives and the conditioning that created it. He stoically accepts his lot as a given, or at best a challenge that the "real man" will accept and cope with and only the "sissy" will not.

These attitudes were brought home to me when I was investigating the interpersonal lives of adult men. I asked them if they had any close male friends. Many seemed surprised by that question. "No. Why? Should I?" was the usual reply. They perceived their isolation, their lack of friendship with other men, as "normal." It was not something even to be questioned or examined.

The lack of close friendships between men may, in part, reflect the fact that they, too, experience the sterility, aridity and superficialty of intimate relationships with each other. How long can conversations about cars, politics, business and sports prove fulfilling and nourishing?

The repression of emotion, the denial and suppression of vulnerability, the compulsive competitiveness, the fear of losing, the anxiety over touching or any other form of sensual display, the controlled intellectualizing, and the general lack of spontaneity and unself-conscious playfulness serve to make the companionship of most men unsatisfying and highly limited. Men are at their best when a task has to be completed, a problem solved, or an enemy battled. Without such a structure, however, anxiety and self-consciousness accelerate too rapidly to allow for a sustained pleasurable experience.

This is also what makes feminist independence a threat. If a man cannot turn to other men in a crisis; if there is no support available to see him through periods of transition and change; if he can only bond comfortably with other men in pursuit of a tangible goal or to defeat a common enemy, he has no basis of intimacy for reaching out to them. It is particularly uncomfortable in moments of weakness, vulnerability, humiliation or pain.

His relationship with his woman is suffocated by the heavy weight of his dependency and draining demandingness, as he turns to her for everything. If she abandons him, his emotional lifeline will have been cut. At the same time, he never clearly defines what it is that he needs or wants from her. He detaches himself, with occasional moments of explosiveness, to control the torrent of unexpressed feelings. She will in turn either come to hate him for it or "suffer through it" masochistically.

Finally, there will be rapid physical decline, because health-giving things are mainly feminine. To take care is not masculine.

Before the age of liberation and feminism he could rationalize this self-destructiveness: He was doing it for his wife and family. That made it all valid and worthwhile. Today the enlightened and honest woman is owning up. "You're not doing it for me: you're doing it for yourself. And if you're doing it for me, please stop, because I'm not getting anything from it. It's boring. It's dead and I hate it."

But the sham is revealed. In spite of the fact that she no longer wants what he is giving her, he can't stop giving it. This is the man who is told by his female companion that she does not want him to intervene or "protect" her in an argument or when a man makes a provocative comment, yet he can't hear her and persists in spite of her wishes. What is clear is that he is doing it for his *own* needs. A former police chief of Los Angeles, noted for his "macho" attitude, a man who liked to call himself the "meanest man in town," revealed this in a recent interview: "Men have the responsibility to protect women in the classical sense—to open the door of the car for ladies." When the interviewer asked, "You still think so today?" he replied, "I still do it. *The heck with them if they don't want it.*"*⁴

As a cardboard Goliath, the male cannot easily shift direction. It was recently reported by Dr. Sandra Bem, based on her extensive research, that "while high masculinity in males has been related to better psychological adjustment during adolescence, it is often accompanied during adulthood by high anxiety, high neuroticism and low self-acceptance. . . . Boys who are strongly masculine and girls who are strongly feminine tend to have lower overall intelligence, lower spatial ability, and show lower creativity."⁵

If he continues to cling to the traditional masculine

* Italics not in original.

blueprint, he will be a victim of himself. He will end his life as a pathetic throwaway, abandoned and asleep. He needs, therefore, to recognize what was aptly described in the ages-old philosophy of Lao-tzu:

> All living growth is pliant
> Until death transfixes it.
> Thus men who have hardened
> Are "kin of death."
> And men who stay soft
> Are "kin of life."[6]

2. The Razor's Edge of Compulsive Masculinity

To be strong, the prisoner once wrote, a man "must be able to stand utterly alone, able to meet and deal with life relying solely upon his own inner resources." To show he was such a man, he once held his hand over a candle flame without flinching. This is G. Gordon Liddy, 46 . . .[1]

It happened on Highway 126 in Fillmore, California, on April 26, 1976. A car with four young men passed another containing three male occupants. The young men in these two cars had never seen each other before.

One of those in the passing car made an obscene gesture at the guys in the passed car. If one is even slightly familiar with the hair-trigger defensiveness of the masculine psyche and the stereotyped, predictable quality of its reactions, the next scene in this freeway drama could be easily predicted.

First, one can easily imagine what went on in the minds of the young men who received this obscene nonverbal communication. "We'll teach those assholes about flipped fingers! No one does that to us and gets away with it!"

Both cars stopped, and there was a fight. Afterward, as the three men drove away, a single shot was fired, and one fifteen-year-old in the passed car was shot in the head. He was dead on arrival at Santa Paula Hospital.[2]

I term this *macho-psychotic behavior*, because it results from what I believe are moments of temporary insanity, those apparently defensive, uncontrollable reflex acts arising from the compulsion to prove one's musculinity.

The incidence of fights and killings in bars and other places where men gather, between individuals whose only contact or communication was an obscene gesture, a slurring remark, a threatening look or some other kind of similar challenge, is high. So commonplace, in fact, that most incidents of this kind rarely find their way into the newspaper.

Supposedly, the drive to survive is the most powerful motivation in the human being. For many men, apparently, this is not so. Rather, the need to prove oneself, "the razor's edge of compulsive masculinity," suffocates the survival instinct and creates a temporary state of insanity when there is a challenge or threat to one's masculinity.

It is important to differentiate at the outset genuine heroics from compulsive proving behavior. Heroic behavior involves an actual danger, or a threatening enemy who intends to harm, and from whom there is no escape. This might be in the form of a fire endangering lives, the rescue of a person in trouble, or protection against someone with clearly destructive intent. However, in the case of the young men in the car, when nothing but the masculine ego was at stake and still life and limb were risked, it is safe to say the persons involved were in a possessed state, temporarily blinded to reason, out of control, out of their minds, and in a *macho-psychotic* condition.

The male driven to prove his masculinity is also in a state of addiction, not much different from the person who is hooked on alcohol or pills. His behavior cannot be affected or changed by logic and reasoning. For example, some therapists have used the tactic of taking alcoholics to the morgue to show them corpses of skid-row alcoholics with their livers eaten away by cirrhosis. The experience has no lasting effect in getting them to stop drinking. So, too, the driven male is beyond reality testing and cannot be affected by the kind of reasoning that tells him he is behaving self-destructively. *In that sense, masculinity can be seen as a psychological defense because it is beyond being affected by reason.*

Tragically, such behavior is only occasionally of an obviously and blatantly self-destructive kind. In most cases, the razor's edge of compulsive masculinity cuts much more subtly, and assumes the mask of hero behavior, and the person is applauded.

One of this country's contemporary economic success stories is a forty-nine-year-old self-made millionaire in CB radios. He had gone through a career in the military and small-time sales before taking a plunge in the business of citizens-band radios, where he went from scratch to a twenty-five-million-dollar business in three years.

A neighbor of his had had open-heart surgery, and one of his friends had a heart attack while driving and wrecked his car. This motivated him to have a physical examination.

His doctor informed him that he was 90 percent blocked. After inquiring about his chances of survival without surgery and being told he would have a maximum of fifteen months of life, he underwent a nine-and-a-half-hour operation.

On the eighth day his wife picked him up from the hospital and said, "You want to go home?" to which he replied, "No, I want to go to the office." Only eight days after major surgery!

In an interview he said, "And now I'm back on the merry-go-round, working harder, longer hours. Traveling more. More stress. More strain. This is just what I shouldn't be doing after my open-heart surgery. But it doesn't seem to be affecting me. I stop every once in a while and say, 'Why am I pushing myself so hard?' And I say, 'Why not? I feel great.' "[3]

On an underlying level, there is an equation between autonomy and masculinity, between overcoming obstacles and resistances and masculinity, between being fearless and all-powerful and masculinity and between not being passive and dependent and masculinity. The need to prove these things supersedes rational self-care and results in compulsive, self-destructive behavior.

The difference between men and women in these areas, between rigidity and fluidity, between compulsive defensiveness and a more reality-oriented response rests in women's greater ability to express strength *or* weakness, independence *or* dependency, activity *or* passivity, rationality *or* emotionality, courage *or* fear, hetero-sensual *or* homo-sensual feelings without threat to their self-image. The man, however, is hooked on his one-track, all-or-nothing response, which appears regardless of the dictates of external reality.

Nowhere does the razor's edge manifest itself in America as clearly, and in such socially approved form, as in the game of football.

The drive in football is enforced at an early age. The "pee-wee pill poppers" are young teen-age boys who go on crash diets of diuretics, laxatives and other pills with possible dangerous side effects in order to lose weight to meet the rigid age-weight classifications. They can then compete in the intermediate divisions, where they stand a better chance to be winners.

One league commissioner reported, "I recall one incident where a kid was so weak from dieting that his father carried him to the scale. I refused to weigh him. Last year I saw one kid slumped on the floor and another who walked around in circles from losing so much weight. They were in too bad shape to be weighed. In both cases the problem was parental. I know of another case where the kid was so weak he contracted pneumonia."[4]

Reinforcement of the compulsion to prove is graphically demonstrated by the appreciative roar of the crowd when a football player is injured or knocked unconscious and returns soon thereafter to the game. It is as if the crowd were saying in unison, "What a man!"

The long-range effects of such "heroics" are being brought out in public for the first time. Until recently, ex-athletes were like ex-soldiers who proudly displayed the wounds they received in battle. To complain or to blame would have cast doubt on their masculinity. Each took it in silence "like a man."

However, some ex-players with lifelong chronic problems received from college football injuries that were not properly treated or given time to heal because the player was needed back in the game are coming forward. Some are filing lawsuits against their coaches, team doctors, or universities.

One player for a leading southern university six years ago was on crutches until just before the game, when his ankle was heavily taped. It wouldn't function, so the team doctor injected it with Novocaine. He then had to have his ankle injected before and during each game for four weeks, because it never got a chance to heal. He now lives in chronic pain from his problems with it.

Another player reports teammates playing with tears

streaming down their faces from pain in damaged knees. But the coaches kept them out there, because the team needed the bodies.

Moses Easley, ex-Indiana football player, said, "You know, as a nineteen-year-old I had all those crazy macho ideas. But it all turned out to be nothing but sadomasochism, walking around all season in bandages. It was crazy. I wish I'd never played football at Indiana."

Andy Lowe, former defensive end for Texas Tech, dislocated his left knee in 1971 and had an operation. He was only supposed to play heavily taped, but his coach didn't like his lateral movements, so they removed the restricting tape. A teammate landed on his knee and Lowe, who is now suing, says, "My leg below the knee just hangs there like a hunk of meat." He may have to have the leg amputated.

Reports on college football players conducted by Dr. Kenneth Clarke at Penn State indicate that for high school and college football players there are 28 significant injuries among every 100 football players. A number of players have indicated that their coaches often instructed them not to tell the team doctors about their injuries, fearing the doctors would order the players sidelined.[5]

The support of early marriage may represent this culture's fear and hatred of unharnessed masculinity. When a very young man marries, to the delight of family and community, are they not breathing a sigh of relief and unwittingly saying, "Another potential animal is off the street"?

A thirty-four-year-old American serving as a mercenary was killed by the Angolan government. He had four children, ranging in age from nine to three and a half, and had been married eleven years. He did it for the money.

His wife commented, "In his own misguided way he was taking care of us. He was a family man." Before he left, he was attending college and working two jobs, maintaining cafeteria equipment and packing parachutes, in addition to serving one weekend a month with the National Guard. He had served in Vietnam.

Despite the fact that he had nailed himself prematurely to the cross of compulsive masculinity, doing all the things "real" and "responsible" men should do, he died in a condition of self-hate, as he described it just before the end.

He wrote his wife: "This will be my last letter to you, because I know I'm going to die. I'm just one of those people who never made good. It will be very hard on you all, and it is all my fault, as most everything that has gone wrong has been. All I can say is that I'm sorry, and I wish I could make it up to you. Please pray that God will let me into his house so that one day I can see you all again. All my love and goodbye."[6] *The priest at the funeral called his wife "an inspiration," but decided against any eulogy for the dead mercenary.*

The man who is obsessed with work, with meeting responsibilities, who drives himself to an early demise after procreating, making money, possibly becoming successful or powerful (most men *never* do!), has lived his life as a sleep-walker in harness. He has equated the compulsively driven need to live up to the masculine imperative with a "meaningful" life.

Even the notion of a man being satisfied because he has "done his work" and feels prepared, therefore, to die may, in an age of expanded consciousness, prove to be another defensive illusion and romantic variation on the theme of compulsive masculinity. The pioneering, creative psychologist Abraham Maslow, known as the father of humanistic psychology, died at the young age of sixty-two. In an interview shortly before his death he spoke introspectively about an earlier heart attack that had come right after he completed what he felt to be an important piece of work. "I had really spent myself. This was the best I could do, and here was not only a good time to die but I was even willing to die . . . it was what David M. Levy called the 'completion of the act.' It was like a good ending, a good close. . . . Partly this was entirely personal and internal and just a matter of feeling good about myself, feeling proud of myself, feeling pleased with myself, self-respecting, self-loving, self-admiring . . ."[7]

The value placed on work as being the ultimate raison d'être of a man's life, as articulated by even this highly respected and sophisticated psychologist, needs to be seriously questioned. Is it perhaps not just another subtle variation on the razor's edge of compulsive masculinity?

Finally the world of fraternity hazing, in which getting accepted by one's "brothers" often involves submitting oneself to humiliation and outright sadism, presents in microcosm the conflict between the external masculine imperative to "act like a man" and the internal craving for intimacy and belonging. It is also an apt metaphor for the dilemma of modern masculinity.

The destructive aspects have been frequently reported by the press. At the University of Wisconsin, a student named David Hoffman died from excessive alcohol consumed at a number of bars while on the "death march," an initiation ritual of his fraternal club. A nineteen-year-old junior at Queens College, going through the rites involved in becoming a member of the Pershing Rifles fraternity, was jabbed with a knife that accidentally plunged through his main artery and killed him. At Michigan State, one senior lost interest in joining a fraternity after he developed a burn on his nose as a result of being forced to rub it along a carpet as part of the initiation rites.[8]

Then there was the Sundowners, a social drinking club at the University of Nevada, Reno, where one man died and another just managed to survive after suffering a complete respiratory arrest subsequent to a bizarre and savage drinking rite that lasted several days and involved the consumption of quarts of tequilla, bourbon, wine, artichoke liquor, gin and so on.

Listen to the tragic explanation of a man who was an honorary pallbearer for the victim, who had played football with him and was tending the bar where the victim had drunk the night he died. He expressed poignantly the distorted manifestations of affectionate expression between men who are psychologically blocked from such direct affectionate display.

"I think the guys quote, unquote who absued him the most were the people who wanted to get to know him and wanted to leave an impression of themselves upon him, to show him that they had a feeling for the club, and they wanted him to possibly have that same feeling. What the witnesses saw was a front. They saw guys yelling and calling bad names, pushing them against the wall, trying to take their hats away. They didn't know the guys liked him. . . . The two who were the most active in John's initiation, I heard one say to the other when it was over, 'I just love the guy.' "[9]

3. Alive at Twenty, a Machine at Thirty, Burned Out by Forty

I've always grown up late. I think a lot of men begin to die when they're in their 20's, when they make a commitment to a fixed life. I was never able to do that. I feel sometimes as though I've never grown up, and I like that. There are still possibilities.[1]

    —Sterling Hayden, actor and author of *Voyage*

There is a notion, or "fact," interpreted as a biological phenomenon but seeming to me to be more psychologically symbolic of the life-constriction process of men, that they reach their sexual peak in their late teens and then go into a decline. Women, however, are said to peak in their late twenties and early thirties.

It is, in fact, one of the tragedies of the rhythm of the male-female developmental process in our culture that men are in the process of shutting down in the same age period when women are unfolding, falling asleep while women are awakening. Consequently, feminine blossoming is met by masculine defensiveness and rigidity. This is manifested more obviously and powerfully today than ever before, as women increasingly give themselves permission to grow into total personhood beyond sex-role stereotypes.

Chris White had been a star athlete in high school and was appointed to a military academy, where he was in officer's training until age twenty-two, when he had to be dropped because of a shattered knee.

In high school and at the academy he was outgoing, had many friends and possessed an easygoing, fun-loving style. After leaving the academy, he married his beautiful high school sweetheart, Donna, who was now building a career in public relations. He took a job with one of the largest, most prestigious encyclopedia sales companies in America.

Though only twenty-three, Chris was already well along in the process of becoming a machine, and his call for help, which clearly took all the courage he could muster (he thought about it for two months before telephoning me), seemed motivated by some unconscious, self-preserving instinct that was pushing him into reexamining himself. He was in painful conflict over things that were going on at his job and in his marriage.

When he arrived for his appointment, he was wearing a gray suit with a vest and tie. His hair was short and perfectly in place, and his overall grooming was impeccable. His manner and speech were careful and conservative. It was hard to believe that he was only twenty-three.

Chris was approaching a stage in the life cycle described in a research article, "Natural History of Male Psychologic Health," co-authored by psychiatrists George E. Vaillant and Charles C. McArthur. According to their study of the male life cycle from age eighteen to fifty, men tended to hustle hard between twenty-five and thirty-five. "Poor at self-reflection, they were not unlike latency children—good at tasks, careful to follow the rules, anxious for promotion, and accepting many aspects of the 'system' and instead worked hard to become specialists."[2]

My patient came to see me, as most conformist males do, with great reluctance and trepidation and *only* because he thought his problems would yield rapidly to clear-cut and usable solutions. He told me that he did not want the bills sent to his home, because he didn't want his wife to know of the visits. He feared it would upset her. It was clear that in his mind one or two hours of talk would take care of everything.

He was in particularly painful conflict about his job, which he initially took because it afforded him the prospect of a lucrative future. His manager was prodding him to begin by selling encyclopedias to his friends, and he found it embarrassing and uncomfortable because, as a result of his sales approach, many of them were beginning to avoid him. His manager insisted, however, that this was the only way to get the ball rolling and become successful. He even urged him to lie and tell his friends that he needed the sales to win a contest.

Equally discomforting was the fact that his manager

had sent him back to his former academy to sell ency-clopedias. The administration at the academy turned him down because of previous bad experiences with other alumni who had returned to campus to sell various prod-ucts. His manager was threatening to file a lawsuit against the academy in order to gain access, claiming that the company's rights were being violated. Chris White felt manipulated, resentful, confused and fearful that he would alienate former friends and acquaintances and get a repu-tation as a troublemaker.

Then there were the problems in his marriage. He loved dogs and wanted to get a German shepherd, but his wife didn't want a dog, so he deferred to her. But inside he deeply resented it.

In addition, there were the times when he had felt par-ticularly troubled and lonesome and wanted his wife to spend the day at home to talk with him and make love, because he had been working evenings and rarely saw her during the week. She refused, explaining that she was in the middle of important projects and was needed at the of-fice. He felt hurt because her job seemed to be more im-portant to her than he was.

Once a fine and enthusiastic athlete, he now spent his weekends at home papering and painting walls and gardening. Though his wife was only twenty-three, like himself, he saw her already developing into a henpecking, dominating person like his mother. Still, he felt too guilty to confront her and reluctant to forcefully assert his needs, because he perceived her as being fragile.

He would meet attractive women during the week who aroused him sexually, and he wanted some freedom, but again he hesitated to discuss this with his wife, because he thought it would "wipe her out." Periodically, he fan-tasized about getting a divorce but rejected the idea be-cause he felt both their parents would be too deeply upset. Besides, everybody had said that they were the perfect couple—attractive, ambitious and bright.

He would come home at night occasionally wishing that his wife had been killed in an automobile accident so that his conflicts could be resolved without guilt. He hated him-self for these thoughts. He was beginning to brim over with anger and frustration but could see no alternative except to use more self-control to overcome these feelings, which he wanted me to help him with quickly.

Like many other men in their early twenties, Chris had directed all of his energies toward "making it" while denying important feelings and needs. Deadening his inner experience and at the same time accommodating himself to externally imposed role expectations that were in opposition to his inner feelings led to machinelike behavior.

By age thirty, most men are well along on the journey of proving themselves and becoming dehumanized "things."

I was recently invited to the thirtieth birthday party of a rising star in the business world—the brother of a close woman friend of mine. The party was attended by members of his football alumni association and some business acquaintances and friends from his army days. The invitation said the gifts were to be funny. As the party was ending and he opened them in pained good humor, the forced "witty" comments of his friends and himself, as well as the gifts, all focused on whether or not he could still "get it up" or "keep it up." The general idea was that at thirty he was over the hill and on the way to becoming an old man.

The men at the party were active sportsmen, and outdoor games could be played in the handsomely decorated, spacious backyard. Instead, they sat around drinking beer and discussing real estate and business.

The powerful decline from age twenty to forty takes place on every level as the man goes from being:

1) Urgently sexual at twenty, to sexually mechanical at thirty, to sexually anxious, defensive and grateful just for being able to perform at forty.

2) Restless, passionate about his ideas, eager to push the limits and experience of his life at twenty, to conservative, "appropriate" and accepting of "reality" at thirty; to holding on tight and just trying to maintain his place at forty.

3) Physically active, energetic and finding pleasure in movement and play at twenty, to exercising purposefully in order to fight his waistline and stay in shape at thirty, to engaging in physical activity at forty, if at all, in a compulsive, serious and measured way, motivated by a fear of heart attacks and other physical ailments.

4) Playful, curious, adventurous and hungry for plea-

sure at twenty, to controlled, with his pleasure outlets limited to dinners out, movies, television, photography and shopping at thirty, to passive and reluctant to try new things or to forsake the sporting event on television at forty.

5) An optimist and laughing boisterously at twenty, to a pragmatist, realistic and with a more inhibited sense of humor, at thirty, to cynical, with a snicker if he laughs at all, at forty.

6) Buddyship oriented and close to male friends who are important to him at twenty, to being more guarded around other men and getting together socially usually only in the company of wives or girl friends at thirty, and at forty in a situation where friendships have evaporated because the men are either divorced, overburdened or living elsewhere and without time or motivation to participate in any close male relationships.

7) Blunt and honest often to the point of rudeness at twenty, to appropriately tactful, phony and manipulative by thirty, to not really knowing what he feels or believes in at forty, because everything has by now been discolored by his overriding motivations of expediency and proving himself.

The roots of this decline are clearly not mysterious, nor need one rationalize these changes as being "normal" passages. In fact, in a self-aware, self-responsible, humanly creative world, I believe that people would scoff at the notion that stages are predetermined and predictable. They would recognize these so-called stages as being nothing but comfortable rationalizations for conformity and loss of mastery over one's existence and developmental pace.

The decline is set in obvious motion in his early twenties *because* he is making critical and often permanent and irreversible life decisions at an age when he is figuratively asleep in terms of his self-awareness and understanding. In his late teens and early twenties he is driven by the external pressures of his culture to prove himself a man, long before he is aware of what it is that he really wants for himself, apart from what he has been told and therefore presumes that he should want. He gets prematurely locked into cages, cornered and trapped in life situations with few, if any, comfortable or apparent options.

It is, in fact, a humanly destructive culture that does not do everything in its power to prolong this early decision-making period. It should prevent the behavior that turns his adult years into something akin to military conscription, in which doing one's duty and paying dues in the form of seriousness, responsibility, adjustment and self-denial are paramount.

To add insult to injury, after he has prematurely locked up and thrown away his life, he may be labeled a chauvinist, an alcoholic, a wife abuser, a manic-depressive or a cold, uninterested family man. He is left defenseless because he hasn't the ability to examine the obvious roots of these expressions of rage and self-hate. He has also not had the supportive psychological climate which would make it possible for him to free himself from the destructive binds that triggered his twisted responses.

Much attention has been paid recently to the "male menopause," the newest rationalization for male deterioration, a process that supposedly occurs in a man's forties and fifties when his functioning starts to break down. This so-called climacteric strikes me as a sort of death rattle, a last glimmer of awareness and cry of protest and pain before the total demise of the self. I personally do not accept the rationalization that the "male menopause" is simply the result of panic over declining potency, biological changes, the fast pace of modern life or the breakdown of traditional values. To my mind it is the noise of the male organism shattering under the weight of oppressive, dehumanized conditioning.

This decline, caused by years of repression and emotional denial, makes him dangerous to others as well as to himself—particularly to his sons and other young men. Because he has placed himself on the cross and endured unending frustration, he has a strong vested belief in and commitment to the values for which he sacrificed himself. It would be threatening indeed for him to acknowledge that he has been a sleepwalker, self-destructively conformist and deluded. His defenses against this awareness will cause him to resent and block the more spontaneous, growth-oriented and meaningful life-style of younger men, which he interprets as irresponsible and adolescent. He will try to thwart it by withholding support so that it cannot be maintained for long without extraordinary effort and ego strength.

He will gladly invest in his son's professional training or back him for a start in business if the money is available, but he won't encourage what he considers an "unproductive" process of self-discovery and an expansive orientation toward life. He wants younger men to pay the same dues he paid, to travel the same road he walked. And the more he has committed himself to his own self-denying style, the more difficult will it be for him to break through the defenses that continuously reassure him about the rightfulness of his behavior.

While many modern women are at least willing to reexamine the time-honored, "sacred" roles of mother and wife that have been their chief source of identity, and also to acknowledge their stifling aspects, men continue to negate their feelings and pretend they are comfortable in their roles. Most probably they cannot perceive any alternatives, because these roles affirm their manliness. And that is *the* important thing. Any changes would threaten that status and arouse intense anxiety.

Some men do escape this process constriction and live a more expressive existence. They are the late-bloomers, the "child men," the creative people—the ones who have never fit into the traditional mold. These men stun with their individuality and are either adored or scorned, considered lusty and free or crazy misfits, depending on whether they have been able to make their style functional and materialistically profitable.

These are men who have found it impossible to conform, because they have never lost touch with the person inside and are therefore not able to regiment themselves into a style that will require them to suppress their individual humanness. The pain and struggle they experience as young men for being deemed misfits or "different" are repaid in the long run, if they find their niche, because they remain more fluid, interesting, sensual, playful, passionate, ever-changing and even charismatic. While other men of their age are withering, they are blossoming and retain a youthful, timeless quality, because they have navigated by their own senses, perceptions and rhythm. They are the Zorbas, the Picassos, the Chaplins and many others who are not well known but who continue to be lusty and who can relate to young and old without an awareness of age difference or consciousness of barriers.

Others who sometimes escape the process of constriction are those who experience a shattering crisis early in life and are able to learn and benefit from it and reorganize their lives in a new and more authentic way. These are men who perhaps had some personal problems and also possessed the openness to reach out for professional help. They opted to stay with their own self-discovery long enough to break through and undo harmful attitudes and reaction patterns that would have otherwise suffocated them.

The point is that no man will escape the inevitable end points if he conforms to the traditional processes of rigid masculine conditioning. These processes and the patterns they generate are overpowering and their consequences inevitable. The conceit of most men is that they feel they *can* make the traditional journey and somehow magically avoid what they have seen occurring in others.

A culture interested in liberating men would slow the life decision-making pace down greatly. Jobs would be seen for what they are; tasks and role behaviors needed to keep the society functioning—not *the* reason for being alive. A young man would be discouraged from establishing permanent relationships early in life and certainly discouraged from fathering until his own identity was well under his conscious awareness and control. Ultimately, the best method of population control would be self-aware, self-caring men who simply would not reproduce early and abundantly, because the price that had to be paid for living under this kind of pressure would obviously be too great. Only fools would risk it.

By becoming self-aware, I believe, he would develop physical and emotional patterns that would greatly extend and expand his life and his youthfulness. There would be less urgency to assume heavy responsibilities early. The pressure of time that many contemporary men feel would be seen as an artifact of the destructive conditioning and early burning out which the masculine game plan produces. His stages or passages would also be revealed to be the penalties for his lack of consciousness.

Self or other abusive behavior, be it alcoholism, child or spouse abuse, indulgence in the purchase of prostitutes as a manifestation of the inability to have the kind of sex life he needs and desires, drugs, compulsive overwork or cynical detachment would be revealed to be symptoms of self-hating, self-destructive, frustrated, trapped male, rather than the chauvinistic "bad boy" behavior of the inherently "evil" man.

4. Sleeping Is Feminine

Ronald Blake was a thirty-nine-year-old radio talk show personality at the time he went into the hospital for a corneal transplant operation. He was known throughout the South as "The Tennessee Iron Man" for his all-night program, which he often conducted without any accompanying guests. It was just he and his call-in listeners. He was at the peak of his career at the time of the surgery. It bothered him that he would be laid up for at least a week after.

His beautiful new wife was at his bedside throughout. Theirs was a brand new marriage, the second for both. She was fourteen years his junior and an aspiring actress-singer.

"I really feel restless," he told her, while chain-smoking in his private room only one day before surgery. "I'm gonna go crazy just lying here. I'll try and talk them into letting me broadcast live from my bed."

The radio station manager loved the idea, because Blake was one of their superstars, and the publicity value of their "Iron Man" broadcasting live from the hospital would be enormous. Nevertheless, he gratuitously asked Blake if he was sure he could handle it and that it wouldn't slow his recovery.

With the adrenalin flowing and his beautiful wife sitting nearby, he boasted, "I feel fantastic. They'll be the greatest shows I've *ever* done. No problem here!"

Being persuasive and charming, he succeeded in getting his doctor and the hospital administration to go along with him, as long as he remained under their constant supervision. The staff thought it would be good public relations for the hospital, which they wanted to have recognized as being a progressive one. It would also help the morale of

29

other patients, many of whom tended to be overly fearful of resuming normal activities after an operation, they rationalized.

Blake loved the idea, too. He would be a model for all of the sick people who wallow in self-pity, and that excited him. He was sure his audience would love him for his courage, and that his audience would grow. It would reinforce his "Iron Man" image and at the same time reassure his wife that she didn't have a middle-aged invalid on her hands.

She brought champagne to his room, and he recruited her to help him with the logistics of the broadcast. It would be good experience for her too because he knew she wanted to break into show business.

Warned that a cold or infection would severely impede and possibly even be disastrous for the healing process, he popped Vitamin C pills continually. When he felt feverish or headachy, he simply increased the dosage, without even discussing that with his physician. He saw himself as an expert on this vitamin, because he'd read a lot about it, so he figured he couldn't go wrong by self-prescribing these "harmless" pills.

Six days later he was discharged from the hospital, and by then he had become "fast friends" with most of the staff. He had proven to everybody that the "Iron Man" label was no hype by turning his recovery into a party without any complaining, self-pity or special attention.

Three months later he collapsed right after his nightly program and was taken to the hospital with double pneumonia. Two years later he died "unexpectedly" and suddenly of a heart attack.

Blame it on the Y chromosome, the supposedly weaker male form, which allegedly makes the male more vulnerable than the female to certain disorders. Or blame it on biological inferiority, or even on man's evolutionary history which has been credited with making the male less well adapted than the female to the contemporary stresses of civilization.

The facts remain that men are far more susceptible to degenerative diseases than women. By 1974, the rate for mortality from malignant neoplasms was 1.49 for men in comparison to women, an increase from 1.08 in 1950. For heart diseases, the mortality rate is more than twice as high. Cerebrovascular disease has risen from a sex mortality ratio of 1.07 in 1950 to a value of 1.21 in 1974.[1] By the next century, it is predicted, men will be living ten years less than women.[2]

It is indeed very much in the masculine psychological tradition to search only externally for the explanations and causes for his physical and emotional problems. The genetic, biological and historical focus turns the issue into an intellectual puzzle, a scientific problem to be solved. Little emphasis is placed on anything that would involve self-awareness, emotions, relationships or psychological introspection. Besides, most men are still pretty well convinced that psychology and the introspective, self-awareness orientation is mystical, tender-minded garbage.

Yet from a psychological perspective, it is both an obvious but subtle and difficult awareness to grasp that the basic processes, attitudes and behavior patterns that are life sustaining and health nurturing are commonly identified as feminine. At the same time, on a physical care level, traditional masculine values and attitudes can be seen as synonymous with physical self-destruction. For example, it is masculine (1) to be able to take as much pain as possible without giving in to it, (2) to hold liquor, (3) to recuperate from serious illness quickly, etc., etc. In fact, there is even something feminine just about being sick in the first place, perhaps because it involves acknowledgment of vulnerability and helplessness. Many men who are ill are embarrassed to acknowledge it and, in fact, will deny it as long as possible. *That's masculine!*

The factors which have resulted in the equation between self-care and femininity have also, I believe, created what I term a *body-psychotic* condition for many men. What that means is they have lost touch with their bodies. In effect, one could say they have *no body*, in the same way the psychotic personality has lost his sense of self, and has *no self*.

The masculine imperative, meaning the pressure to live up to the mandates of masculinity, has caused him to lose his body awareness. As a little boy, he was taught to tune out body signals and to perceive certain attitudes toward his body and his health as masculine, while others were considered sissyish or feminine. Consequently, it is not uncommon to find workaholic middle-aged men, alcoholic, hyperactive, overeaters who are chronically driven. These are the men who tell you they "feel great" one day, and then "suddenly" fall prey to a major illness or even drop dead the next.

This lack of awareness of their physical deterioration, while engaged in the most obviously self-destructive of habit patterns, is a manifestation of the *body-psychotic* condition. *Stress, self-poisoning, fatigue and emotional pain do not register.* Their early conditioning as men has numbed that awareness and made it anxiety provoking to give in to them even when they *do* experience it. These men are detached from the voice of their body. They do not experience the body's growing signals of distress and the accumulation of dis-ease, until they break down altogether.

It is pathetically ironic that the very characteristics that constitute the heart-attack-prone Type-A personality, the personality and response configuration of the man most likely to succumb, are the same characteristics that have been said to lead to success. They include being highly competitive, compulsive about deadlines and quotas, being highly achievement-oriented and pushing oneself constantly. He has been written about as follows: "The Type-A person works hard and fast to succeed, and in striving toward his goals he suppresses feelings such as fatigue that might interfere with his performance. Type-A's get angry if someone or something else gets in the way of their success . . . rises to master challenges out of a need to control the world."[8]

To embarrass such a man, telephone him in the afternoon, and say, "I hope I didn't wake you from a nap." "I wasn't sleeping!" will most probably be his quick and defensive reply in a guilty tone, or one which would suggest that you had impugned his manliness. Or even telephone him very early in the morning and apologize for having awakened him. "I've been up for quite a while," "I wasn't asleep," or "I was just about to get up" will probably be his reply. It will be most important for him to *deny* that he'd been asleep.

He reacts like a little boy who has been caught stealing. Guilty! He has been caught napping, "asleep at the wheel." He feels accused of nonmasculine behavior. Gently ask him on the freeway, after a long stretch of driving, if he'd like you to take over because he looks tired. "No, I'm fine! I'll let you know when I've had it." Then he will continue to deny and fight his fatigue as long as possible.

Sleeping is feminine because sleeping is a passive activity. Passivity equals femininity. During sex, for example, the man is traditionally supposed to be on top and active while the woman is supposed to be on the bottom, more reactive than active and in traditional feminine behavior, passive and submissive.

Because passivity equals femininity, passivity might also unconsciously equal homosexuality. On the deepest level, particularly for the most masculinely defensive of men the unconscious equation might be seen as follows: Sleeping equals passivity, passivity equals femininity, femininity in a man equals homosexuality; therefore sleeping, beyond a certain minimal point, would be equated with homosexuality. Consequently, it could be predicted that the more macho the male, the more uncomfortable he would be with long stretches of sleeping, taking of naps, inactivity or any forms of passivity or "doing nothing." A typically macho attorney, describing the difference in attitude between himself and his wife, said, "Sleeping is a necessity. She likes to lie in bed in the morning. I like to get up early." When he's in trial, he often gets up as early as 2:30 A.M. "I like to get ready to do battle. I'm never happier than when I'm in court," he said.

In fact, most men would proudly tell you how little sleep they need in order to function. The unspoken message is, "See how masculine I am!" The scientist who could develop a pill that would allow men to go without sleep altogether would undoubtedly become an instant billionaire.

Sleeping conjures up other, more consciously negative associations such as laziness. There is the inner voice of past authority warning him as a boy always to be doing something and, particularly, not to sleep his life away. "Do you want to spend a third or more of your life sleeping?" He does not see sleep as enriching and extending his life, in quality and quantity, but rather as being a waste of it.

The masculine psychological imperative does not allow him the psychological space to grasp what Shakespeare so aptly perceived, when he wrote in *Macbeth:* [4]

> . . . Sleep that knits up the
> ravell'd sleave of care,
> The death of each day's life,
> sore labour's bath.
> Balm of hurt minds,
> great nature's second course,
> *Chief nourisher in life's feast.**

His conditioning, his anxieties and his compulsions even prevent him from fully experiencing his need for sleep. He may become an organism without a passivity cycle, and in this way he is unlike any other organism. For years he blocks out the fatigue, kicks himself back into activity as he would a tired horse, and to accomplish this he uses pills, cigarettes, coffee, liquor, stimulating diets, vitamins and whatever else will allow him to deceive his body into suppressing its exhaustion.

The result is that he ages and burns out prematurely. But in the short run, being able to do with little sleep is a triumph and a habit that he feels will keep him one step ahead of the crowd, a winner! By age forty he is already a physical caricature of his younger self; paunchy, balding, wrinkled, with poor eyesight and general physical enervation manifested by various aches and pains. Rather than reveling in good body feelings, he is now physically defensive, obsessed with heart-attack prevention, weight reduction, reducing his drinking and maintaining his potency.

His resistance to passivity also ties in with his goal orientation. That is, he won't do something if it doesn't have a purpose because he can't afford to "waste his time." As one young man so aptly expressed this orientation, "I can't even take a walk without feeling I'm wasting my time. If I'm not going somewhere specific or for a reason, I feel

* Italics not in original.

uncomfortable. I have a constant gnawing feeling of anxiety and guilt."

When he exercises, it is also for a purpose: to keep in shape. When he touches a woman, it is for a purpose: to have sex. When he has a lunch date, that too has a purpose: business and making money. And when he plays or otherwise spends time with his child, it is for a purpose: to make sure the child is exposed to the right things, to ease his own guilt over not being an involved parent and to pay his dues and reassure himself he is fulfilling his responsibilities as a father.

Because passivity is feminine, everything, including his greatest pleasures, eventually becomes a job because he is always goal oriented. He plays to win, so playing becomes a form of stress. When he doesn't play as well as he "used to," he might stop playing altogether, because he didn't play for the fun of it originally so there is no point in playing if he will lose. When he makes love, as the dominant one, he must have an erection. Failing that, as he someday must, what was once pleasure will become a source of anxiety, a terror and a job.

Not only is sleeping feminine, but it is a part of the self-destructive nature of masculinity that the healing, recuperative, life- and health-sustaining attitudes and processes are essentially considered feminine, while body-destructive attitudes are considered masculine.

1) *Emotional expression is feminine.*

Women are emotional; men are supposed to control themselves. So men's emotions undergo repression, and they fall victim to stress-induced, psychosomatic illnesses.

2) *Giving in to pain is feminine.*

Boxers, though bleeding and half conscious, stay in the ring and fight until they're forced by the referee to quit. Even then they will protest the call if they have *anything* left at all. Or, as one football coach told his limping player as he urged him to continue, "I've never seen a guy die from a sprained ankle." To another, he remarked, "You play with the small hurts, boy!"[5]

The male learns to equate his masculinity with his ability to take pain. The equation he lives by is a simple one. "The more pain I can take without giving in, the more manly I am." Only after the cumulative symptoms have become so great that they throw him over, does he give in to them and only then because he has to. He can disown personal responsibility and blame the illness. "*It* knocked me flat."

3) *Asking for help is feminine.*

He drives around the neighborhood for a half hour rather than pulling over to ask for help with the directions. When he's hurting, often nobody knows. "I don't want to impose on or bother anybody," he says. The feelings of discomfort he experiences when asking for help outweighs the benefits he believes he'll receive. On a deeper level, he may be asking himself the painful question: "Am I lovable when I'm not strong and healthy?"

A recent research study showed that although 65 percent of psychiatrists asked said that they saw more women professionally, 77 percent added that they didn't see more women who actually required psychiatric treatment. According to the researchers, that seemed to indicate that men don't make their first appointment until their symptoms become really severe. Women feel culturally freer to seek help because for a woman it is not viewed as an admission of weakness.[6]

4) *Paying too much attention to diet, especially when you're not sick, is feminine.*

He has been taught, and he believes, that because he's a man he needs to eat more heavily, even if, in fact, his work is less physically exerting than the woman's. Therefore, although he sits behind a desk all day in his office, he eats like a warrior embarking on a two-week hunt.

Eating meat is masculine. Perhaps it is the association of meat with blood. He has been told that the great warriors of old drank blood. Facts do not deter his magical belief in the idea of meat proteins making him strong, even though recent research indicates that "the only thing produced by excess intake of protein is high performance urine," and that protein is not a good source of energy because it has to go through many complex biochemical changes before becoming available as an energy source. Nor does additional protein enhance physiological work performance.[7]

Not only is it a myth that extra protein gives strength,

but a diet high in meat and dairy products, along with refined flour and sugar, has been tied to six of the ten leading causes of death in the United States, including heart diseases and certain kinds of cancer.[8] Recently, when the U.S. government put two hundred obese rats on strict protein diets similar to those blamed for the deaths of sixteen women, 95 percent died within a month.[9]

5) *Alcohol abstinence is feminine.*

In many small towns across America, the fear of reflecting negatively on one's masculinity by not drinking in the company of one's male friends, almost every evening after work, is far greater than any concern about what the alcohol is doing to the body. Drinking, after all, is *the* primary basis for men relating to each other socially and of proving their masculinity. Again the equation he learns is simple and blatantly self-destructive. "The more liquor I can hold, the more masculine I am."

Never mind that recent studies show that alcohol enhances the carcinogenic impact of other agents, so that alcoholics are more prone to mouth, throat and liver cancers.[10] Or that cirrhosis, brain damage, vitamin deficiencies, premature aging and a significantly shortened life span are other results of regular alcohol consumption.

It is a reflection on the interpersonal anxieties and the limited capacity of men to find satisfying sober pleasures in their life, that they need the liquor *in spite* of what they know it will do to them.

6) *Self-care is feminine.*

Pampering oneself, taking long, leisurely baths, exploring oneself in front of the mirror, going to health spas, and taking "beauty rests" are all "feminine" activities. Men have "more important" things to do, namely, working and being otherwise productive. A man who is unduly involved with his physical well-being is suspect. He is labeled narcissistic, effete, a hypochondriac or worse. Conversely, the man who is the most reckless in attitude toward his physical well-being is seen as being most masculine.

7) *Dependency is feminine.*

Getting sick often means having to let other people take care of you. Letting other people take care of you, worse still, expecting them to, is feminine. The man who can stand alone, does not rely on others, expresses no dependency and is least needful is the most manly.

8) *Touching is feminine.*

The nourishing, healing and comforting roles of touching are well documented in psychological literature. But touching, especially when it is purposeless (meaning it is not a prelude to sex or a formal greeting), arouses the man's anxiety and makes most men uncomfortable.

He learns that lesson early. Asking to be cuddled, held, kissed, stroked, rocked is for girls. Boys shake hands and that's about all the physical contact they share unless they're celebrating a victory, and then a pat on the ass or an arm around the shoulder is acceptable. A barber interviewed in a film about men called *Men's Lives* commented, "For many men, the only time they get any touching is when they come in here."[11]

So his body is tense and he looks to inanimate outlets for relaxation, such as eating, drinking liquor, watching television, etc. The human touch is acceptable only when it is for a purpose, such as a massage to "loosen his muscles," or touching before intercourse, mainly to loosen *her* up and to make *her* feel good. Otherwise, he is a rare, pathetic species in this world, one who has learned through conditioning that being touched is taboo because touching is "feminine."

In summary, masculinity in the care of the body means:

1) The less sleep I need,
2) The more pain I can take,
3) The more alcohol I can hold,
4) The less I concern myself with what I eat,
5) The less I ask anybody for help or depend on them,
6) The more I control and repress my emotions,
7) The less attention I pay to myself physically, *the more masculine I am.*

It is basically futile to warn or preach to a man that he should rest more, eat or smoke less, express emotions, etc. Like the neurotic who needs his symptoms to preserve his psychological balance, the man makes an unconscious equation between self-care and femininity, and he will therefore resist and ultimately abandon and subvert the most sincere intentions and efforts to change.

A typical conscious masculine rationalization for avoiding a change in self-caring behavior patterns is, "Why should I stop? I might get killed crossing the street, or get hit by a falling rock. So I'll live a few years less. At least I'll be enjoying myself when I'm here." Or "I don't want to be a 'health nut.' "

The changes, if they are to come, must emerge from a reclamation of his total self, the consciousness of himself as a whole person. As long as passivity, emotions, dependency, self-care, etc. equal femininity in his conditioning, while self-destructive proving and the tuning out of and learning to deny and overcome body messages is masculine, warnings and beseechments will fail. He, himself, must realize this conditioning and refuse to self-destruct just to prove himself. The awareness of what he has allowed to happen to himself, however, must come first. Resistance to following a self-destructive course in order to live up to an image could then follow.

He who can risk change, and reclaim the right to self-care and experience the satisfaction and pleasure of physical self-awareness and health, will never again return to self-destructive patterns. The body's signals of protest and the bad feelings he would experience when he behaves self-destructively would act as a constant, haunting reminder. And the incredible pleasure of being in tune with rather than the victim of his body would replace the momentary validation of his masculinity afforded by his former physical self-destructiveness.

5. The "Secrets" of Success

Judging from the continual flow of books on the subject, there is an insatiable appetite for literature on the techniques and secrets of becoming successful. Many of these books allege to lay bare the eternal, hidden, unspoken truths of life and human motivation, the attitudes required for "making it," the stuff that others dare not speak or will not reveal and that will open the palace doors to gold and riches.

The philosophies expounded range from inspirational, positive thinking, "pep-talk" approaches to various jungle philosophies that spell out in endless variation the cynical themes: "It's a dog-eat-dog world." "Do unto others before they do unto you." "Altruism is naïveté." "Every person is only out for himself," or a la Machiavelli, "The nature of men is such that most forget more easily the death of their fathers than the loss of their property."

The real "secret" of writing and publishing these books is that there exists in most people a belief in the illusion of techniques, a seemingly eternal, unshakable fantasy of the existence of a "magic key," a perfect formula, a combination of moves and strategies that will unlock the doors to success. Due to this propensity, there can exist at the very same time, widely read, popular books which offer totally contradictory advice and philosophies. Each manages to find its own group of ardent, convinced supporters.

The "secrets of success" that cannot be taught are deeply ingrained personality traits. These qualities, when combined with a specific skill or outlet or direction, and sound intelligence will almost assuredly produce success. These ingredients include:

1) *Basic Distrust*: These men keep their own counsel, increasingly so as they climb the success ladder. They reveal their inner life to no one. Perhaps they are unknown even to themselves. For them, trusting is naïveté and dangerous vulnerability. It is the kind of human interaction that they believe will only interfere with and possibly sabotage their upward mobility.

Their unspoken philosophy, the one behind their surface cordiality and attentive and polite facade, was perhaps best articulated by George Smiley, the fallen chief of British intelligence in *The Honourable Schoolboy*, a spy novel by John Le Carré:

> . . . I have learned to interpret the whole of life in terms of conspiracy. That is the sword I have lived by, and . . . the sword I shall die by as well. These people terrify me, but I am one of them. If they stab me in the back, then at least that is the judgment of my peers.[1]

2) *Need to Control*: A counterpart of *basic distrust* is the *need to control*. This need allows one to avoid vulnerability and spontaneity and is also intrinsic to the traditional masculine style.

The highly aggressive, success-driven man has it to an extreme. He will avoid situations and people he cannot control. Eventually, his relationships are reduced to business-related ones. "Best friends" are his accountant, lawyer, business manager, etc. His wife, who is probably in the background, is appropriately submissive in relation to him. In his personal relationships, he is more or less obviously a tyrant, and the unspoken, reigning rule is: "Do it my way or leave."

Relationships which are not readily controlled and which result in conflict or excessive demands on his personal time are systematically eliminated.

3) *Manipulation*: He treats people as objects for manipulation.

One part of this orientation was cogently expressed by Dorothy Schiff, one-time owner, publisher and sole stockholder of the *New York Post,* and for many years one of America's most powerful women. In a published interview she commented, "Most people to me are nothing but personnel problems."[2]

Discussing her personal life, she commented, "Unforeseen problems always arise in my marriages. Maybe very common problems, but they always take me by surprise." When the interviewer asked her what sort of problems she was referring to, she replied, "That the other person has needs . . ."[3]

Extremely goal oriented as part of his pursuit of success, the success-driven man operates in detached, rational fashion, without allowing feelings, his own or those of others, to interfere.

According to some researchers, this approach is even prerequisite for the successful empire-building style. Psychologists David C. McClelland and David H. Burnham, in an article titled, "Good Guys Make Bum Bosses," pointed out that a bad boss is "a man whose main drive is for affiliation—to be friendly with everyone, including the people who work for him. His desire to be liked leads him into wishy-washy decisions, and he cares more about the happiness of particular individuals than the well-being of the whole working group."[4]

Social-industrial psychologist Jay Hall expressed it this way: "Good managers challenge their people; poor ones comfort them."[5]

The qualities of men who create effective organizations which expand into empire bases are described in the psychological book *Power: The Inner Experience.*[6] They include:

1) a strong need for power
2) a weak need for affiliation
3) a strong need for control

Manipulation, turning off one's human side in order to get results and reach a goal, is very much a constant part of a young boy's conditioning in our culture. He is rewarded for *winning,* nor for *caring.* Caring, he is taught, is the province of women, the territory of the Red Cross nurse. He learns also that an excellent grade in school or a triumph in sports is applauded and remembered, while the process involved in getting it is not. In other words, it's not so much a case of "What did you learn?" but "What grade did you get?", not so much "How you won," but "Did you win?"

Translated into everyday behavior, *manipulation* means that when someone else has something to offer that is desired or needed, involvement with and interest in that person is strong. A person who is not needed, however, becomes invisible. Relationships are cultivated and maintained for their usefulness. People are extensions of objects, used for specific purposes and then discarded or set aside until the need for them arises again.

Like *basic distrust, manipulation* as a style of relating is a deeply rooted part of the personality. It emerges from early conditioning experiences which put the primary focus on achievement, goal orientation and winning. He learned that only total control spelled safety, and that "love" was contingent on being successful. Some have more of that dehumanized jungle ability to manipulate than others. It cannot really be taught because it is not a question of a handful of moves but is rather a constant, all-pervasive style that is always in operation.

4) *Repression of Human Needs*: Dr. Thomas Stockmann, the maverick of Henrik Ibsen's *An Enemy of the People*, expressed his style as follows: "I am one of the strongest men in the world . . . the strongest man in the world is he who stands most alone."[7]

Repression of human needs, coupled with intelligence and drive, would allow a man to become a fine achieving performer, a well-oiled machine. Without the intrusion of human needs for physical and emotional contact and interaction, a man can comfortably obsess himself and his work in his office, laboratory, shop or wherever his success drive is being nurtured, and work a fifteen-hour-a-day, seven-days-a-week schedule. Not only is intimate human contact not required, but nongoal-oriented activities and people involvement are seen as an intrusion, an irritant, an obstacle to bypass as quickly as possible.

His social life is an instrument for his success. His wife and children are a part of his career building. Dinner, social engagements and trips become increasingly more business connected and purposeful. Otherwise, vacations and weekends are a waste of time at best, dreaded at worst.

He navigates as a "winner" must; self-controlled, logical, detached and decisive. The success drive engulfs everything and his life-style becomes a triumph over intimacy.

He disconnects from those people in his life who don't facilitate his goal. A troubled child of his, or a wife with emotional problems puts him into a particularly difficult conflict. He cannot easily fire them or deny their existence. If it would work, and if he could, he would hire his own resident psychiatrist to attend to that uncontrollable part of his life.

In general, as personal contact becomes more intrusive and annoying at home, he would verbalize his feelings as follows, if he were being transparently honest:

1) Let the housekeeper take the kids to the zoo.

2) Use your vibrator for your damn orgasm if you're frustrated.

3) Talk to a shrink if you've got a problem.

4) Take a class in the evening if you need something to do.

5) Send the kids to boarding school if they won't shape up.

For himself, the words "I need" on an intimate level choke in his throat before they can be expressed. *Need* is not to be felt and certainly not to be exposed. He is locked into his posture and as he becomes increasingly invested in it, it becomes ever more threatening to examine and get in touch with deeper needs.

More success and more power become increasingly easier to pursue and acquire, because all other activities are less comfortable for him. To be a workaholic is his refuge. It protects him from an awareness of the dehumanized life he has created. Rather than enjoying the benefits of the success he has acquired as he originally imagined he would, all he really ends up feeling comfortable with is more work and more success.

Success-driven men are fiercely goal oriented. They are machines in acceleration and with no brakes. They are men who finally can stop only by crashing, physically or emotionally.

They pay the price with their humanness. By middle age, they have become isolated islands unto themselves. Their emotions have been submerged and only surface occasionally, usually in erratic outbursts of anger or frustration. They become increasingly more rigid in their need to control others, and distrustful to the point that they expose themselves to no one. Relationships are segmentalized, meaning that people are related to in terms of the function they perform rather than as whole individuals.

The sudden mood swings and eruptions, alternating between rage and depression and so common in men who reach the loftier heights of success, can be interpreted as the inner life voice experiencing annihilation and screaming, out of control, to inform him that his humanness is being consumed.

If he can avoid a psychological encounter with his inner life and handle the turbulence with stabilizing drugs, he will. Success-driven physicians, equally as phobic about encountering themselves, will accommodate his need to avoid self-recognition. Many of them can understand and empathize with his style very well, because they share it.

In the end, the rewards of his success are revealed as masturbatory. There is really no one to share them with when he gets "there," no one close enough who really cares or knows him and whom he genuinely trusts and feels close to. The satisfactions of the success are, in the main, only symbolic. Control over others, money, renown are his, but they are all just a part of the preparation for living. Originally seeking out the success and power to make himself safe from a threatening world, he barricades himself to the point that not only is he protected from the "dangers" but he is shut out from the whole process of living itself.

Our society is full of success-driven men at the end points of their success voyage, living in a nightmarish world of not knowing whom to trust, unable to find satisfaction in intimate contact, unaware of what they want and feel, and rigidly resistant to opening up in order to find out.

While achievement and accomplishment are important

for a sense of self worth in most people, the success-driven man has substituted the acquisition of symbols for human intimacy and satisfaction. In a psychologically aware society, such a life-style would not be praised or respected but would be recognized for its dehumanized quality and its destructive impact on the person himself and those around him. It would be seen for what it is, a pathological, dangerous disorder.

6. Afraid to Fail, Even at Suicide

There is a statistic the meaning of which, once understood, illuminates one of the deepest and most powerful aspects and motivations of masculine behavior. The implications of it are at once far-reaching, pathetic and chilling.

Women attempt suicide at least four times as often as men. The disparity is probably larger, because women tend to attempt suicide with milder means than men, preferring pills, for example, to guns. Many of these attempts therefore are not recognized as such and are not officially recorded. Men, however, *succeed* at suicide close to three times more often than women. Put another way, nearly 90 percent of suicide *attempts* are by women, whereas over 70 percent of *completed* suicides are by men. Again, the difference is probably greater, because many male suicides are probably disguised as accidents—for example, automobile accidents.

This disparity in suicides increases considerably with age. While men at all ages commit suicide at rates approximately three times higher, by age sixty the rate for successful suicides is at least five times as high for men. Also, men of sixty or older kill themselves at rates approximately four times greater than men under twenty.

Clearly, for the male, age does not bring security, wisdom, serenity, mellowness and philosophical acceptance. The depiction of grandfather on the porch, contentedly rocking and smoking his pipe, is a romanticized distortion. Aging makes men psychologically *more* vulnerable, brittle and prone to self-destruction.

The suicide attempt has often been interpreted by those in the helping professions as an indirect "cry for help." *This interpretation, however, is generally true for women only.* The man who sets out to commit suicide means to achieve it. A study of methods employed by male suicides showed that in over 50 percent of cases firearms were used, while approximately 20 percent were by hanging.[1] Suicide-prevention centers report that they get at least twice as many calls for help from women. One male registered nurse at a Los Angeles mental-health center, who works with the suicidal male and female over the hot line and directly in his ward, reported that many men will use guns or knives and tell him over the phone that they have these weapons at hand. Other popular masculine methods, according to him, are jumping off buildings or driving off a cliff. He therefore becomes more alarmed when a man calls up, because he will more than likely go through with the act.

The tragic element in masculine role conditioning is that crying for help is considered feminine behavior. When a man is confronted with overwhelming problems and pain, it is very difficult for him to admit his inadequacy. Asking for help is not an appropriate masculine approach, so when the situation becomes unbearable, only one solution is possible: death.

A study by Kate Frankenthal, M.D., pointed out this inter-sex difference in a recent report for the Sixth International Conference for Suicide Prevention. Women attempt suicide as a cry for help, and such demonstration of weakness is fitting. However, the man has been taught that masculinity requires that he face death fearlessly. So when he contemplates suicide, he is going to succeed and "die like a man."*[2] *In other words, even at the moment of self-destruction he is under the same pressure to succeed and not to fail.*

He is thus caught in an impossible bind. If he asks for help, he impugns his masculinity. If he goes it alone, he crumbles under the weight. The latter is apparently preferable for most men. So instead of reaching out, he quietly gets his life in order, pays the bills, checks on his insurance and tries to exit in a way that won't be an imposition on anybody. The fact that he prefers death to impugning his masculine self-image is the most telling comment about the nature and self-destructive power of his conditioning.

* Quotation marks not in original.

Once one grasps the insidious and deeply self-destructive nature and meaning of his conditioning, one can see how it would be a great humiliation for him if he happened to survive his suicide attempt. First, he would have to face what he would interpret as the scorn of those who knew him and would condemn him for having "copped out." Second, he might have to acknowledge and deal with the very feelings (fear, rage, vulnerability) that drove him to it. Confronting one's inner emotions is a dreadful threat. Third, and as frightening for him, he might only wound himself and survive as an invalid. In his mind, this would make him a dependent and hated burden, because all of his life he felt lovable for being the strong man and the caretaker whom others could depend on. Finally, he would jeopardize his future employability. Without a job, he believes, he would be better off dead.

One study showed that 15 percent of the people who committed suicide had received but not followed a recommendation for psychiatric hospitalization within a few weeks of their death. Men apparently resisted it because it would mean a loss of earnings. They feared that the psychiatric label would make them unemployable in the future.[3]

In a paper by Harry Levinson titled "On Executive Suicide," published in the *Harvard Business Review*, the author pointed out that when a highly successful man is at the end of his rope, he must not admit to having problems and must not under any circumstances give way or seek help. In fact, to seek help from a friend or the company doctor is considered a sign of weakness and failure to cope. Moreover, if he seeks help from a psychiatrist or a psychologist, he will fear being seen as either weak or crazy or both. "When a conscientious executive with tremendous self-demands recognizes that he is failing to cope effectively with a situation under circumstances in which he must control intense negative feelings, he may see limited alternatives. If he does not seek professional help, escape from an apparently hopeless situation can seem possible only by developing psychosomatic symptoms, by attacking himself in the form of accidents or, in the extreme, by committing suicide."[4]

It is traditional in our society, which depicts the male as

"top dog," to account for the devastating male statistics, namely, significantly shorter life span, significantly higher disease and death rates, and a preponderance of emotional problems in boys, with biological or genetic explanations. This has even been done in the case of suicide, where one psychological researcher-theoretician rationalized the higher suicide rate in men as reflecting a general biological law that the male clings to life less and is less resistant to stress than the female.[5]

One need not conjecture further about this kind of explanation once it is recognized how deeply embedded the fear of failure is in the male. As a young boy, he is repeatedly given the message that success and winning make him lovable and worthwhile. There is hardly a more devastating label than that of "loser." Some boys get the message in an extreme form through their father's rejection and his intensely negative reaction when they do poorly. Indirectly, the boy gets the message because he is adored when he triumphs. He also observes the powerfully positive reaction of his parents to other boys when *they* are successful winners or prove themselves to be the "best." These early evaluations contaminate his pleasure in many activities as he grows older. If he can't win or do very well at something, he won't do it at all. This progressively narrows his range of involvements until he winds up as primarily a spectator to most activities except those in which he can excel.

One study on the phenomenon of "skidding" and "occupational mobility" described the possible connection between suicide and failure at work. Most men identify themselves with their occupations. When achievement at work goes badly, so does their self-image. One hundred and five consecutive male suicides in a large southern city were studied by a Tulane University sociologist. He found that:

1) Among the suicides, considerable downward mobility ("skidding") was found and relatively little upward mobility.

2) Decreasing incomes characterized more than half the suicides, whereas men of the experimental control groups (non-suicides) were showing gains.

3) When the occupational level of the suicide and his

father were compared, considerable mobility, mostly downward, was discovered.

The researcher commented, "It is not difficult to form the impression that these men felt acute dissatisfaction with their performance and standing in their respective business and professional circles."[6]

The fear of failure infects and ultimately destroys every man who has not succeeded in wresting himself from its powerful grip. Most important, it prevents him from ever discovering what it is he really *wants*, because what he *doesn't* want is so much more powerful a force in his life. *He doesn't want to fail.*

Because of this phenomenon, he is unable to learn and benefit from his experiences of failure except to search for ways to avoid future failure. That is, when problems arise at work, in a relationship, sexually or even in competitive activities, he cannot read the potentially health-giving, growthful messages that may exist in the failure of his resistance. His organism may simply be shouting, "No!" or "Get me out of here!" However, he cannot read the "No!" All he hears is the encroaching, haunting chorus chanting the word "failure." So he hangs in when he should let go, tries to succeed when his resistance is overwhelming, while struggling at the same time to avoid self-loathing.

The deeply embedded fear of failure also makes every victory one that is short-lived and essentially hollow, because each success, more than representing an accomplishment, is an avoidance of non-success or failure. Therefore, on a deeper level, *each important success makes important failure that much more imminent,* because each important success raises his standard of performance expectation that much higher. The level of yesterday's success becomes today's level of failure. Those who become extremely wealthy and successful, motivated by the need to prove themselves, to perform and conversely, therefore, by the fear of failure, become the most vulnerable. One highly successful motion-picture director expressed this succinctly: "With each film it gets worse—and this is my tenth film. The waiting is awful. When I started directing I told myself it'd get easier with each film. It doesn't. In the beginning it was easier because I was just happy to be working."[7]

As far back as 1954 the late and noted psychiatrist Dr. Don Jackson reported in his paper on suicide for the *Scientific American*, "Professional people commit suicide more commonly than nonprofessionals, white collar workers than laborers, officers than enlisted men."[8]

It is commonly noted that many men who become rich and highly successful are not able to let go and enjoy the fruits of their work. If anything, as they become successful and wealthy they seem even more driven, more compulsive in their work routines than when they were poor.[9] The more open and aware among them often comment that, indeed, life tasted better and they enjoyed themselves more when they had less.

Of course! At their new pinnacle so much more energy is required just to maintain the new level of failure avoidance, because *anything* but *more* represents failure. So the pressure increases, their pace quickens, and if there is nothing to interrupt them, their road all too often ends in either interpersonal isolation, a heart attack, alcoholism, an emotional breakdown or the collapse of everything they put together.

Once this underlying motivational dynamic is recognized, the often defensive and enclosed behavior of the powerful, the successful and the wealthy person becomes easier to understand. It also becomes clearer why the rate of suicide among older men increases so dramatically and out of proportion to women of the same age and to younger men. At an age when, so mythology tells us, wisdom and comfortable detachment should be in operation, the experience of failure becomes that much more inevitable and pervasive. Previous successes, no matter how great, provide no cushion.

When the fear of failure is a stronger motivator than the desire to grow, a psychological time bomb becomes embedded within the masculine conditioning, a disease process that makes every traditionally brought up male a potential suicide in one way or another.

The self-caring man will not react in a terrorized way to failure of any kind. Instead, he will embrace it for its potentially important self-revealing messages. Failure in a relationship would be seen as a growth-yielding, freeing end. A resistant penis would be seen as a signal to explore and take responsibility for real feelings toward the person he makes love to. Failure in his job would show him how he might be misdirecting his energy. Even illness would be welcomed for its information about self-destructive habits that need to be corrected.

Once he is free to value himself for his capacity to live his life fully, rather than simply perform and avoid failure, others will relate to him accordingly. The fear of failure will no longer serve as a criterion for the way he evaluates himself. Its removal, however, will not be an easy process, because it has become so much a part of the way he acts. But, once liberated, he will cease to focus on how people react to his level of success.

7. The Impostor Fantasy

I felt like a fraud.
So I learned to fly an airplane.
At 50,000 feet I thought:
"A fraud is flying an airplane."
So I crossed the Atlantic in a rowboat.
I docked at Cherbourg and thought:
"A fraud has crossed the Atlantic in a rowboat."
So I took a space shot to the moon.
On the trip home I thought:
"A fraud has circled the moon."
So I took a full page ad in the newspaper and
    confessed to the world that I was a fraud!
I read the ad and I thought:
"A fraud is pretending to be honest."[1]

—Jules Feiffer

A thirty-three-year-old New York attorney is admired and acclaimed for his activist-humanistic orientation, specifically, the pains and risks he takes helping migrant farm workers and non-English-speaking prisoners with their legal problems. For no financial compensation and on his own time, he also writes and distributes a newsletter that reports on police and judicial abuses in the treatment of these aliens.

Speaking during one of his moments of self-loathing, he confessed, "People think of me as a humanist, a guy who cares. Basically, I think most of the men I work with and help are a bunch of schmucks. They're assholes as far as I'm concerned. I'm really doing this for *me*, not *them*. My public image is of a 'together' white dude, not just another phony liberal or closet racist. But half the time, when I'm talking to myself, I'm thinking, 'That lazy nigger!' or 'That dumb Chicano!' "

However, it disturbed and haunted him to think that he might be a phony, because he had always been an idealist. But now he was beginning to feel like an impostor and was considering quitting his job, even though his work was still admired and he was considered one of the very best at what he did. "I don't know if I can go on living with myself this way," he said.

A thirty-eight-year-old psychologist committed suicide. For a number of months before he killed himself, he had become increasingly depressed about his work. His wife reported that he would ruminate out loud in a self-hating, depressed tone. "I'm *not* the wise old man with answers. I'm *not* what people see in me. I'm sitting in my office listening to people and they'll be crying, and I can't get into their pain no matter how hard I work at it. All I can think is, 'That's tough shit! I'm sorry you're feeling bad, but so does the whole world. Everybody's anxious or depressed. That's just the way it is.' "

He was obsessed with the idea that he had no right to continue being a therapist. In fact, it began to feel impossible to him even to pretend, and his self-hate increased until it became unbearable.

Similarly, a child and family counselor, well known for his fine theoretical publications on the dynamics of family life and childhood problems, found himself with a failing marriage, a drinking problem, and a twenty-year-old son who was into hard drugs. The thought, "How come my family and personal life is so messed up when I'm supposed to have all the answers?" tortured him. "What if the families I worked with knew all this?" he thought. "I'd probably have no practice."

A motorcycle policeman was arrested for masturbating near his motorcycle while "peeping" into the bedroom window of an attractive stewardess. He talked about himself to the psychiatrist he was sent to see by his attorney. "For years I've been making drug arrests and hiding the fact that I was heavily into marijuana. I'd go to parties not knowing whether to smoke a joint, and I know even my friends wondered if I was going to bust them. When I was twenty-two I had a sixteen-year-old girl friend who I went to bed with. Now, that's statutory rape, right? I'd do crackdowns on porno places, but I've enjoyed my share of porno films. It's been driving me crazy—being two people—a cop and the real me. Maybe I had to blow it this way, and do something crazy to save my sanity."

A forty-seven-year-old orthopedic surgeon, with an additional graduate degree in biochemistry, was the director of his own clinic and the administrator of a small hospital. In spite of his extensive education and training, he was obsessed with the fear that he would someday be revealed as an ignorant poseur. "During a case conference I'll be sitting there terrified that someone's going to ask me some questions and discover that I don't know *anything*."

His fear of being "revealed" intensified when he made the decision not to devote as much time to his work and instead to spend more time studying classical guitar and being with his three young children. Rather than enjoying this, he became increasingly frightened that he'd soon be professionally obsolete and make a fool of himself and be forced out of his medical group.

He was particularly intimidated by an older colleague who arrived at work every morning at six-thirty and spent an hour and a half reading medical journals. He felt certain that this colleague would eventually see through him and find out that he wasn't keeping up. While he had rarely received anything but very favorable feedback about his work, he continued to be haunted by his feeling of being an impostor, to the point that he tried to befriend everyone in his clinic, from other doctors to the nurses and aides. He reasoned that he would be safer if everybody liked him and would be on his side when he was finally exposed.

A thirty-seven-year-old political-science instructor remarked, "I don't really know whether I care about the things I say or not. I've been told I lecture and write with a lot of passion, but actually I don't even know what I really believe in. I do know it's publish or perish, so I put on paper what I know will get published. As far as I'm concerned, most of it is just shit, but I'm playing the game. I might as well be selling shoes, though, when it comes right down to it."

A television newscaster in a large eastern city was earning ninety thousand dollars a year as an anchorman. His drinking problem, however, was getting worse, and he decided to quit and take a job in a smaller West Coast city for considerably less money. "All the while . . . I kept thinking, 'Someday they're going to find out that there's a thousand guys out there who can do the job better, and how do I keep them from finding out?' It was a constant strain."

And the young owner of a health-food store expressed a feeling that I've heard from many men: "There are two voices inside of me," he said. "One voice says I'm brilliant, sensitive and the greatest. The other voice says that I'm a total con, a bullshit artist and everybody can see through me. Once upon a time I really believed in health foods—fresh fruits, wholesome breads, nuts. Now all I want to do is sell the vitamins, because that's where the money is, even though I know most vitamins do nothing but feed on people's suggestibility and wishful thinking."

On a self-assessment questionnaire about masculinity that I distribute to men who come to my lectures, there is one statement they are asked to answer as to whether it is true of them. The statement reads, "I often secretly feel like a phony or an impostor at work, like I'm faking it, and that sooner or later I'll be found out."

A large number of men from a wide variety of professions—engineers, planners, safety specialists, firemen, naval flight officers, physicians, computer scientists and so on—answer yes to this question. The impostor fantasy, the feeling that one is faking one's job, that one is the opposite of the image one projects, and the fear of being exposed that results, is a common experience.

These impostor fantasies take various forms. The "intellectual impostor fantasy" involves feelings of having fooled people into believing one knows far more than one really knows, and fearing that one will someday be revealed as ignorant.

The "role impostor fantasy" involves feelings that one is faking one's commitment to one's job: "I'm not really dedicated like they think I am. I act enthusiastic, but I don't really believe in the product I'm selling. I'm not committed to the welfare of this company."

The "personality impostor fantasy" is expressed in

feelings such as: "I'm not really the nice guy I come on as. I'm not the stable, mature, together and happily married man they think I am, and I'm not the sensitive, concerned, self-sacrificing person I present myself as." Behind this feeling is often another one which says, "Basically I'm just out for myself and they don't know it."

The "emotional impostor fantasy" involves the sense that one is projecting feelings to specific individuals that one really does not feel. "The people I work with think I like them, but really I see them as boring and stupid. I wouldn't spend a minute with any of them if I didn't have to." A doctor said, for example, "I don't really care about my patients like I seem to." Likewise, a salesman confessed, "My customers are just accounts to me—they're not even people, even though they think I'm their best friend."

Finally, there is the "role-conflict impostor fantasy," illustrated by one teacher's feeling that he expounds and is supposed to symbolize values, beliefs and commitments to his students that are not at all what he really believes or how he really sees things. One counselor commented, "I teach people to be open to communication and honest with their feelings, but I don't do it myself. I don't even know if I believe it is a good thing."

In all of these instances, the men were haunted by the fantasy that their *real* feelings, the *real* person underneath, would one day be exposed. *These men were not conscious or evil manipulators. Rather, they were individuals caught in a conflict between what they were and what their image said they were supposed to be.*

The impostor fantasy is rooted partly in the belief that to assume certain roles one must acquire certain kinds of feelings. The person playing the role himself believes this to be true and tries to match his identity to the role requirement. For example, good doctors are "supposed to" feel dedicated, caring and self-sacrificing; clergymen are "not supposed to" have carnal appetites, materialistic motivations, hateful feelings and so on. They are "supposed to" have loving, spiritual feelings.

These role images are also reinforced by associating the role with a certain specific mode of dress, speech, grooming and manners. Imagine for a minute the reaction of the public to a president who was giving a speech while unshaven and standing in his jockey shorts, or a gynecologist who smiled and made jokes while he examined a patient. The job might be performed at a high level of competence, but the "inappropriate" accompanying aspects would be totally disorienting.

A psychologically aware society might applaud a political candidate who openly acknowledged his pleasure and appetite for power, money and glory, and who frankly communicated his personal prejudices regarding certain races and religions. He would thus be acknowledging his humanness and he could then be evaulated on the basis of his ability to do the job rather than on his ability to project the required image. Instead, there remains a childlike craving to believe there are superhuman men, that politicians, for example, have no prejudices and are motivated by their concern and love for the people, and we are repeatedly disillusioned because, rather than being beyond "base" human motivations, they are, in fact, heavily mired in them.

The belief in the "good," "selfless," "pure" person who has transcended human emotion and frailty is one that not only dehumanizes relationships but creates endless problems and a highly destructive potential, and at the same time blocks psychological growth. It is much like the woman who never gives up her belief in the existence of the "perfect man," her Prince Charming, and is therefore repeatedly attracted either to men who *seem* to her to be that way but inevitably fall short, or to manipulators who know how to give her what she wants for a short time, to their advantage, and who then abandon her, leaving her with deep hurt, increasing cynicism and a sense of futility about *all* relationships.

Her continued pursuit of this "perfect man" prevents her from ever learning to deal with the problems inherent in relating to real men. In addition, it ultimately dooms her to isolation and prevents her from growing into reality. Likewise, society's belief in the "bigger than life" personality in any role makes it constantly vulnerable either to ruthless manipulation or repeated disillusionment. Either way, cynicism and a sense of hopelessness intensify, while growth is aborted and psychological reality is avoided.

The height of role-expectation insanity was reached during President Carter's election campaign. His election potential was significantly jeopardized when he acknowledged having "lust in his heart." That this statement was even considered a disturbing admission in a society that has made the movie *Deep Throat* one of the largest box-office successes in history and that constantly uses sexual symbolism to advertise and sell many of its products is astounding. But we want our political heroes to fit our role fantasies and to *pretend* rather than to be.

Role-impostor problems are complicated by the fact that men in our society are psychologically isolated from each other, secretive and ready to use another man's self-exposure and vulnerabilities to their advantage. This isolation produces in a man the feeling that he is the only one who has a certain problem, or that he is different or "sicker" than others because of experiencing emotions and thoughts that he believes other men don't have. Liberated, caring and humanized men would applaud and vigorously support the man who exposed his real feelings, fantasies, experiences and conflicts, *no matter what they were*, and would reject those who used such self-exposure to their advantage. The act of opening oneself up would be seen as an act of faith and trust that provides a basis and a beginning for humane bonding among men.

I have heard professionals from a wide variety of fields comment that they do not like to socialize with men in their own profession because the experience is boring and unpleasurable. When I was a fledgling psychologist, I remember my own self-consciousness at parties and professional gatherings as I worried about saying or doing something that would betray personal hang-ups. I felt that I was supposed to be free of them because I was a psychologist. I had the feeling that I would be analyzed, evaluated and criticized if I let my guard down. Apparently, many of my peers had similar feelings, because the atmosphere at social events tended to be cautious and stilted, and the conversation consisted of impersonal intellectualization and role posturing. Any professional gathering where people behave according to their prescribed roles inevitably becomes a constricted and unfulfilling experience.

Perhaps the most frightening possibility in all of this is

that some men have actually repressed their own identity and replaced it with their role image. These are men whose wives and children even refer to them as Doctor, Judge, General or Mister. Invariably, they are respected and perhaps beloved by those who relate to them professionally, while they drive their intimates "crazy" because their responses are always impersonally "correct," controlled and in keeping with their image. It shuts intimates out, and the emotionally unreal communications that result are laden with underlying, repressed emotions the role player is not aware of. My belief is that the more a person has assumed his role as a constant identity, the more emotionally troubled his intimates, wife and children will be.

There are some who consciously and healthfully realize that when it comes to their role, they must be in this world but not of it. They know what the acceptable role behavior is, play the game out of necessity but do not judge themselves for being "phony." Other men who experience impostor fantasies, however, torture themselves with self-loathing. The latter group are closer to humanness and self-awareness than the third group of men who wear their role mantle comfortably and without conflict and experience only what they are "supposed to" experience. Their role and personal identity have merged into one. In fact, it would seem that any man who still had a semblance of humanness and who had not been swallowed up by his role image would experience impostor feelings, because no person with an identity of his own could be what his role dictated he should be. After all, role expectations and demands are static, while human emotions are not.

In effect, those who do not experience a conflict between their inner experience and what their role dictates that inner experience should be have been consumed by the demands of their role. They are role robots, effective performers, perhaps, and therefore socially laudable, but destructive on a human level because of their machineline, out-of-touch behavior. Children of these role players have to struggle for sheer emotional survival in the face of counterfeit responses. They become confused and disturbed by a father who is socially highly respected but is unable to be real beyond his role, and who never realizes what his personal impact is until the children manifest emotional problems. These may take the form of drug addiction, sexual acting out, nervous breakdowns or suicide attempts. They are indications of a child's need to call himself to his father's attention, to reach him emotionally and to free himself from the annihilating interaction.

My physical appearance is a youthful one, and my dress is casual. I struggled for many years with the knowledge that prospective patients would be intimidated by this. I knew that many of them would want their psychotherapist to have a mature, conservative, "father figure" type of appearance, a person who "looked like" a doctor. I toyed with the idea of growing a beard, wearing a suit and tie, or even horn-rimmed glasses, though my eyes were perfect. I realized, however, that I would be committing a kind of psychological suicide, to say nothing of reinforcing an orientation that *causes* emotional problems, and that any success I gained on that basis would be at the cost of my humanness and the patient's potential for ever seeing beyond stereotypes, role images and authority poses. The need to see and believe in the professional as being in a certain mold and somehow larger than life, a father figure, is to my mind a major stumbling block to psychological growth and also prevents patients from trusting in and drawing on their own resources.

By insisting that professionals dress and behave in predictably role-appropriate ways, we reinforce and perpetuate an atmosphere that will ultimately reward either the most manipulative men (in other words, those who are most skillful at "seeming") or those who have actually repressed their own identity and humanness and replaced it with role-required image behavior.

The impostor fantasy seems to me to be the beginning of a role identity crisis that can lead to important human growth. Indeed, it has been my experience that those who suffer the most from impostor feelings are, in fact, potentially the most real. Those who are the most comfortable with themselves as role players have, in effect, become unreal people and have committed an identity suicide.

The impostor fantasy indicates that there is an experienced gap, an awareness of a difference between externally imposed role expectations (the "supposed to be") and the internal experience of oneself. The feelings of being on the verge of a breakdown that the impostor fantasy may generate—"My act is falling apart"; "I can't play the game anymore"—may actually be a healthy resistance to remaining a "role thing." It may be a critical moment of potential growth, even though it is terrifying, because it suggests the fear of losing the protection and security the role and "uniform" provide.

To *feel* like your role, therefore, is a form of insanity: a loss of self. It means that one has replaced one's own fluid self with a stagnant, externally imposed set of behaviors and reactions. This may be equally true when that role is a nonprofessional one, such as "good husband," "good father," "good provider," "strong man" and so on.

Parents of disturbed children, for example, are rarely irresponsible, overtly hostile people. More often they are individuals rigidly working at playing out their role as "good parents," while on a deeper level they contain a hurricane of repressed resentment, resistance, anger and even murderous rage—all of the "not supposed to" feelings that are being blocked out because they are threatening for the role image of the "good parent" to acknowledge. Every communication of theirs, therefore, becomes a loaded, confusing one consisting of the "correct," "loving" response on the surface and the angry, rejecting emotional one underneath which is transmitted in various forms through nonverbal communication and body-language. The child is bombarded with a flood of "push-pull," "come here-go away," "I love you—I hate you" messages. It is literally a "love that destroys," and the child would ultimately be emotionally far healthier if he received an overt message such as, "I hate being your father and I wish you were dead." The child might grow up angry and feeling rejected, but would probably not grow up crazy. He would at least know his reality, even though it was a painful one. So long as intimates and society are punitive in response to a person who has feelings he is "not supposed to" have, emotional repression, hiding, hypocrisy and crazy-making communication will be perpetuated.

Men have been victims of image strangulation because

their social attractiveness and lovability have so commonly been linked with their roles and success. The role-oriented male must continue to successfully live up to his image in order to retain his attractiveness. The prospect of not being able to maintain this becomes terrifying. It spells the end of being lovable. Maintaining a role image, however, seals one into receiving a false, image love. It is one of the most excruciating impossible binds that men face.

Role behavior and the human experience, which seem to have become so powerfully merged, need to be separated. The liberated man would react just as negatively to his attractiveness being contingent on his role as an aware, liberated woman would to her attractiveness as a person being measured by her breast size or her figure. In a society interested in humanness and not in performing puppets, we would applaud the person who resists playing out role stereotypes and who is transparent and open with his changing feelings, hostilities, fantasies and prejudices. Otherwise, we are asking for, and will continue to get, a society run by successful manipulators, role poseurs or role robots, and we will experience all the shock, pain and insanity that are inevitably the price.

In a human society a person who became his role would be the object of pity and revulsion because of having become a human aberration, diseased at best, a dangerous monster at worst. There would be no "great men" with clay feet, because we would know that any man who had become "larger than life" was a human fraud, be he the great religious leader, healer, teacher, poet or whatever. It has traditionally been society's insanity that it believed people could really *be* their image and still be human.

Despair, anxiety, fears of a breakdown and suicidal impulses may occur when the gap between role requirements and personal feelings increases and creates the impostor fantasy. However, the existence of this fantasy must be accepted as an inevitable phenomenon and in a human society we would encourage and embrace this experience as the beginning of a process which would allow the person *esse quam videri,* to be, rather than to seem.

PART TWO

HE
AND SHE

8. The Actor and the Reactor; or Why She Can Label Him Exploiter, Oppressor and Chauvinist Pig

The traditionally socialized woman has had to deny and repress her aggression, her autonomy and her sexuality. The process of doing this begins at a very young age, so that her inability to experience, express and assume responsibility for these important parts of her humanness is largely beyond her conscious control. For example, it wasn't until recent years that most women could even acknowledge their *own* sexual drive—an inner-originated impulse, need or "horniness"—the way men traditionally have. Hers was typically a *reactive* sexuality. She "did it" *for him*, or *he* "turned her on."

This orientation was both the bane and the glory of married men in times past. While she was perhaps never quite the sexual partner he imagined for himself, he was assured that she would not walk around during the day getting turned on by other men. It made him feel safe to know she wasn't a sexual being in her own right. In his eyes, sex with her was a gift, a token of appreciation, a sacrifice, payment made for being protected and provided for or simply an expression of her love for him.

Traditionally she also did not experience or act out her aggression directly. Her identification was with fragility and weakness. She was the passive, peaceful one. In times of danger or challenge he aggressed for her. She was the cheerleader on the sidelines while her football-playing man fought it out on the football field, or she was the Red Cross nurse waiting with coffee, sandwiches, bandages and sympathy when he faltered, fell exhausted or staggered wounded from battle. Helplessness and dependency were her mode and were a part of being feminine.

The business of getting a "Mr. Right" meant marrying

the most ambitious, worldly, aggressive, successful and powerful man she could. He would then take control, make decisions and be the dominant figure. In return he received reinforcement from her, ranging from adoration to affirmation of his masculinity. He knew he had a "good woman" if she still reacted lovingly even when he failed. Her part of the contract was that she would not threaten him by competing with him or making him look bad in the eyes of other men.

In essence, she was trained to be the *reactor* in her relationship with him. That is, he would initiate or take responsibility and she would react to his ability to do so. He led, she followed. He dominated, she submitted. He made the sexual advances, she reacted to them. He owned his sexuality, his aggression and his autonomy. She disowned hers. *He was the actor. She was the reactor.*

This interaction, which traditionally continued throughout their lifetime in various forms, was launched and given momentum early in the courtship ritual. In it we can see the basis for the traditional male-female interaction. In spite of feminist consciousness, androgyny advocacy, ERA and the like, most of these time-honored *actor-reactor* transactions in the courtship phase are still alive and visible.

This is the way it goes. He sees her and is attracted to her. At a party, on the street, in an elevator, a classroom or wherever they chance to meet. Perhaps she notices him too and is also attracted. Nevertheless, it will be his responsibility to initiate the opening conversation. Then she signals her interest through her reactions. If she is very interested, she will be animated and enthusiastic. Less interested, she will be more guarded in her responses. Hardly or not interested at all, she will look through him as if he didn't exist or, worse still, through her reaction make him feel like an inappropriate intruder. He needs to be able to read these signals correctly, because it will again be his responsibility as the *actor* to say, "I'd like to see you. May I have your telephone number?" The rejection, if he has misjudged her degree of interest, is uncomfortable at best.

If he has not misread her and she gives him her telephone number, he breathes a deep sigh of relief and feels pleasure, particularly if he is very attracted and is imagining that she might be THE ONE, potentially his MAGIC LADY. The knot in his stomach loosens and a burst of adrenaline pours through his bloodstream, creating a euphoric anticipation. "I think she likes me," he says to himself.

If he's really turned on, however, this feeling of relaxation and joy will soon be mingled with anxiety and apprehension. He has only passed a perfunctory screening exam and there will be many more tests to come.

He has her phone number and is feeling that he'd like to call her immediately. However, that might make him seem too desperate, too lonely and hungry, which he believes would be a sure turn-off for her. He doesn't want to behave as if there was no one else in his life until he met her. To acknowledge such neediness is very "unmasculine."

He calculates that he'll wait at least two days before calling. Two days is enough time for him not to appear too eager and not so long that she is likely to have forgotten his name or met someone else important to her in the meantime. So he waits. Each hour seems long until the time he can finally call, pretending casualness and nonchalance when he does. After a few minutes of time-filling, time-killing conversation, he says, "I'd like to take you out." Particularly if he believes he's competing for a much sought after prize, he will suggest Friday or even Thursday evening, because it would be too great a risk if he asked her out for Saturday night, the night usually reserved for THE SPECIAL PERSON, if one exists. If she said no, he might not know how to interpret it. "Is she *really* busy on Saturday night, or does she *really* mean that she *really* doesn't want to see me?" he will wonder.

While he's asking her about Friday, perhaps trying to convince her by telling her about the places he'd like to take her, the tension in his stomach increases until she finally answers. The knot then becomes either a flash of despair or a jolt of further anticipatory excitement.

If she says yes and his fantasies of a magical experience have been ignited, he begins scouring the newspaper and his memory for "exciting" things to do, impressive places to eat, and he thinks about what clothes to wear that will make him most attractive. Sometime before the date he may even get his car washed and take a few workouts so that his body will have that extra little definition that makes him look more masculine and appealing.

Comes the evening—and as will be the case throughout the courtship except for special circumstances or under emergency conditions—he will get into his automobile and drive to pick her up. This is taken for granted, even though most women have cars and driver's licenses and driving is not a particularly hazardous activity requiring "masculine" skills. Nevertheless, probably because it is his mandate to be in control, a leader, it also translates into his being the driver. The man who says to his prospective date, "Would you pick me up?" risks his image and may be seen as imposing or insulting. ("He's taking me for granted. He doesn't even care enough to make the effort to pick me up.") Besides, his car is part of his image, an extension of his identity and often a part of the armament at his disposal to excite and seduce her with. The commanding way he drives demonstrates his way of being.

Occasionally this ritual of "picking her up" assumes ludicrous proportions, such as when she lives a good distance away and he has to drive to her house only to bring her back to the part of town he lives in for dinner, then drive her back home before returning to his. The driving part of the date has taken on the trappings of a part-time job.

He arrives at her place at the agreed-upon time, and the *actor-reactor* interaction, if we are looking at the traditional male-female pattern, begins to manifest itself in all of its unbalanced glory.

As a "democratic" *actor*, he says to her, "What would you like to eat?" If she is a genuine *reactor*, she will reply, "It doesn't really matter," or she will throw it back to him by saying, "What would *you* like to eat?" At this point he's in a double-bind dilemma. If he makes the decision unilaterally, he may appear too quick and selfish. If he continues the discussion, he risks appearing indecisive.

His compromise ploy is to use a fairly safe alternative. He may say something like, "How about Italian or Chinese?" However, if she is a heavily conditioned *reactor*, she might answer this one by saying, "They both sound good," or "Either one—I really have no preference," at which point he will recognize the necessity for taking matters in hand. He says, "Let's go to an Italian restaurant.

Do you have a favorite one?" to which a *reactor* might again reply. "It doesn't really matter that much," or "There's lots of places I like," or even more probably, "Not particularly, do you?" A motivated *actor* comes prepared. "I know a neat little intimate place I'm sure you'd like. It's run by an Italian family—just a hole in the wall, but the food's great. It's called Mamma Giovanni's and it's on River Street." She responds with enthusiasm, "That sounds great!" So they get into his car and drive off.

The loaded and ironic aspects of being the *actor* now become even clearer, because during the meal he will feel as ego-involved with the quality of the food as if he had cooked it. In other words, if she really likes it, he'll feel good about himself because *he* made the choice, and therefore sees it as reflecting on *him* favorably as a person. However, if the food is poor, the service slow or the decor unattractive and she reacts negatively, he will take it personally and might feel that much less attractive to her because of it.

After the meal, the check arrives. His date may well be an aware, independent and liberated woman whom he would not dare relate to in old-fashioned, chauvinistic ways. Nevertheless, he is unable to raise the issue of payment be it the first or fifth date, or to simply say, "The bill comes to thirteen dollars; that's six-fifty for you and six-fifty for me plus money for a tip." It would sound rude and make him look cheap, even if she is at about the same income level as he is.

Contemporary advice columns dealing with this often inform men that they should not feel offended or see it as a rejection if a woman insists on paying her share. The option, however, is still seen as hers. None of these writers point out how preposterous it is in this age of liberation for it to be taken for granted that payment is his responsibility. Nevertheless, even when he is with a woman he knows to be liberated, he would find it uncomfortable and generally out of the question to confront this issue head-on. To be seen as "cheap" is to be unsexy and unlovable. The waiter even colludes with this as he hands the man the check, face down, as if the whole business was dirty and the woman was not to be involved with such a low-level matter.

My objection to this is not regarding the act of a man's paying for a woman, particularly if his income significantly exceeds hers. Rather, I react to the presumption that payment is his responsibility and that this is taken for granted and only altered at her insistence.

Back to the date. The check is paid, and now he's faced with the second major dilemma of the evening: what to do after dinner. He says to her, "What would you like to do now?" to which, as a *reactor*, she is likely to reply, "I don't know," or "What do you suggest?"

Again he chooses and pays, and again, if the movie or the nightclub or any other activity is *his* choice, his principal concern will be, "Is she enjoying this? Did I make a good choice?" Again it is the phenomenon of his identifying with the choice and feeling responsible for its quality. A good movie means that he's sensitive and tasteful. A boring movie means that he's not. Good music means that he's cultured and aware. If she doesn't like the music, he feels that his judgment is faulty and she won't like him.

Added to all of this, throughout the evening he might also be straining to generate and maintain interesting conversation. He sees it as his responsibility to keep her entertained in every way, even in creating a stimulating conversational flow.

If he's still very excited about her at the end of the evening, experiencing her as special, he might be looking for a sign that she is also attracted to him, be it through a spontaneous holding of his hand, putting her head on his shoulder or kissing him. If he is like most single men in our society, he is starving for affection, touching, intimacy and feedback that tell him he's lovable. While these needs of his are repressed most of the time, they get unleashed when he is in the midst of the fantasy that he has found *the* woman for him.

During the drive home, he tries to interpret her behavior. Is she sitting near the door (that means she's not turned on), or is she moving close to him (that means she likes him)? Is she talking in animated fashion (that means she's interested and wants to connect), or is she yawning and seeming to be tired (that means she's not)? Is she telling him that she has to get up the following morning at 6:30 A.M. for a ten-mile Sierra Club hike (that means goodbye at the door), or is she expressing delight at the prospects of a leisurely, lounging day tomorrow (that means he'll be invited in)?

Sometimes the signals are mixed and confusing and require acuity to interpret them. That is, she may be sitting close to him but yawning at the same time, or she might be engaging in animated conversation while she sits tight up against the door.

His signal-reading ability had better be accurate, because he is particularly vulnerable in the sexual area. If he comes on to her and she responds with delight, then he'll be floating, suddenly transformed in his eyes into the most attractive man in the world. If she responds coldly, however, and with an attitude that seems to be saying, "What are you doing?" he will flood himself with self-hating messages and name-calling: "I really blew it with my impatience and aggressiveness." Echoes of past accusations may then reverberate inside him: "Horny! Insensitive! All you really want is sex!"

The *actor-reactor* model has been set in motion. Throughout, he has assumed the role of *actor* by initiating the date, making the choices, paying, asserting himself sexually and so on. With only occasional exception, unless she is a nontraditional woman, she has been reacting, positively if she is turned on and interested, negatively if she isn't.

The evening's interplay is crucial to an understanding of the bedrock of the male-female interaction. It exposes the roots and reveals the reasons why a woman today can righteously point accusingly at a man and in bottomless-well fashion assert that he is responsible for every heinous crime and exploitation while she paints herself as an innocent victim. That is, *Reactors are never guilty. Actors are responsible. Therefore, only actors can be portrayed as evil or exploitative.*

Actors are either heroes or bums, liberators or destroyers, winners or losers, and sooner or later every man falters, fails or falls, at which time he will stand accused while his latent self-hate, guilt and negative self-accusations will reinforce this sense of responsibility.

In its extreme form, the experience is comparable to that of an impressionable lay person in the company of a clergyman. The latter behaves as if he had no animal impulses, no animosities, no anger or hate, no selfishness or materialistic desires. This inevitably incites self-conscious feelings of being inferior, sinful, undeveloped, dirty and so on in the lay person. Likewise, the woman who, for example, does not acknowledge her own sexual hungers can generate feelings of being animalistic, horny, insensitive and boorish in the typical guilt-prone male who does express these desires.

It is this *actor-reactor* dynamic that has made it possible for feminist writers to accuse men of driving women crazy or exploiting and abusing them. Passive-submissive role players, be they male or female, always end up feeling used and "pushed around," until one day they scream out, "You're not going to do *this* to *me* anymore!"

Even enlightened, psychologically sophisticated and educated male writers and professionals fall into the trap of not recognizing the loaded quality of this dynamic and accuse themselves and other men. For example, according to Ashley Montagu, in his book *The Natural Superiority of Women*:

> 1) Woman is the creator and fosterer of life; man has been the mechanizer and destroyer of life.

> 2) Women love the human race; men behave as if they were, on the whole, hostile to it.

> 3) It is the function of women to teach men how to be human.

> 4) Because women have had to be unselfish, forbearing, self-sacrificing and maternal, they possess a deeper understanding than men of what it means to be human.

> 5) By comparison with the deep involvement of women in living, men appear to be only superficially engaged. Compare the love of a male for a female with the love of the female for the male. It is the difference between a rivulet and a great, deep ocean.[1]

Psychiatrist Dr. Lester Gelb wrote an essay entitled "Masculinity-Femininity: A Study in Imposed Inequality."

In it he wrote, "It took me many years to realize that when a woman described many of the men who wanted to take her out as 'no damn good,' she was likely to be right."[2]

The *actor-reactor* interaction causes the man to appear to be an exploiter and also generates feelings in him of being responsible for the woman's happiness or unhappiness. For example, the following excerpt from the book *Divorced in America*, by Joseph Epstein, illustrates a man's feelings toward his ex-wife:

> You had had a letter from their mother, now your ex-wife, two days ago. In it she explained having come up with some mysterious female problem. One sentence in the letter affected you particularly. "Whenever I am away from you for any length of time," she wrote, "I seem to become sick." You wired her two hundred dollars through Western Union yesterday morning, for this illness would keep her from working for a week or so. Wavering between guilt and anger, between fantasies of reconciliation and vengeance, your feelings toward your ex-wife seemed beyond sorting. For the most part, you felt awful about her. You ardently wished she would remarry soon and solidly, to a wealthy, intelligent, gentle, tolerant man—in part because you really wanted good things to happen to her, *but in even greater part so that you could at last stop worrying about what exact share you had in the unhappiness of her life."*[3]

The more powerful his need for control and dominance, the more vulnerable he is to being portrayed in this way as a bad guy. David G. Winter of Wesleyan University, Abigail J. Stewart of Boston University and David C. McClelland of Harvard University recently studied the relationship of power-motivated husbands and their submissive wives. They concluded: "The power-motivated man, it appears, not only tends to distrust and exploit women in fantasy and through adolescent sexual 'con-

* Italics not in original.

quests,' he also appears to suppress them (or their career aspirations) in real life."[4]

This is just another of the endless examples of what eminent researchers repeatedly conclude: *He is the heavy. She is the innocent.*

Because the male has owned and acted out his sexuality, his aggression and his autonomy, he has inevitably set himself up for being the target for all the vile accusations currently being hurled at him. Because he has not been able to see beyond the surface interpretations, he is a bottomless well of guilt, self-hate and confusion. It will be discussed and demonstrated farther on in this book that women are just as sexual, potentially as aggressive and even more independent of the male than he is of her, and that *actor-reactor* role playing enhances every masculine self-destructive tendency and reinforces all of the female illusions of being the innocent victim of exploitation and abuse.

In actuality, in the *actor-reactor* interaction ultimate power resides in the *reactor*, who is very much like a Skinnerian behavior modifier shaping the behavior of a pigeon in a cage. (Skinnerian psychologists influence behavior by determining which acts shall be rewarded and which shall be punished.)

In the male-female interaction of *actor* and *reactor*, the process of interplay is basically unconscious on both sides because of the intensive early conditioning process and therefore its processes need to be rooted out by making them conscious. They need to be put into perspective primarily because the *actor* role is such a lethal and loaded one. So long as he continues to play that role, he will be haunted by latent or overt feelings of being responsible, even if he has lost everything and wallows as a skid-row alcoholic or is a divorced, lonesome, desperate soul living in a one-room apartment while his ex-wife continues apart from him in the mode in which they lived when married. He will still be filled with self-hate and images of himself as having been the destructive one.

In less drastic instances, the role of *actor* still causes many husbands to engage in self-hating ruminations that run something like this: "I don't know how she puts up with me. She has the patience and soul of an angel."

By playing *actor* to her as a *reactor*, he has actually

given her considerable power and control over him. He looks to her to affirm his lovability. Often his evaluation of his behavior is tied to her reaction. If he is a success and she applauds, he feels validated. In some instances, even while the money he earns is readily spent, he still receives negative feedback for his low-level preoccupation with making money and the kinds of people he associates with in his working world, or for the fact that his ambition deprives the family of his involvement.

If he experiences failure, she may be supportive or she may react in a rejecting way, as many men have discovered when their women turned cold as their business failed or they were fired from their job. Whether she reacts with love and sympathy or with hostility and rejection, the point remains that his reaction to himself is often intimately linked to her reaction to him as an *actor*. This makes him extremely vulnerable.

Likewise, the traditional male sees it as his role to be the woman's protector, even though she is often in no danger and may not even desire "protection." He will risk health and life, for example, to battle another man who makes an offensive remark or a pass at "his" woman.

In the sexual arena, too, by being the initiator and the active one, if his performance falters and he gets no erection or fails to facilitate an orgasm for her, he floods himself with doubts and negative evaluations and looks to see if she will continue to care about him and be patient while *he* works *his* problem out.

By his lack of consciousness in these matters, he digs his own grave. The gun is surely loaded. By clinging to the role of *actor*, he sets the stage for his inevitable nightmare.

The female role of *reactor*, while allowing her to escape the punishment of being an *actor*, must ultimately be frustrating to her as well. The fact that she knows she can indirectly control and affect his reactions must overwhelm and at the same time revolt her. To see a man apologize and cringe in pathetic self-hate because he doesn't have an erection or because he lost money in an investment or was fired from a job must, on a deeper level, make it very difficult—if not impossible—for her to feel really good and loving toward him.

Furthermore, as the passive-submissive *reactor*, she has

had to deny critical parts of herself and has thus built up a reservoir of rage. The rage accumulates because, by adapting to the rhythm and identity of the man she is involved with, she is denying and crushing so much of herself. Inevitably, she will see herself as being exploited, someone who is there just to service his needs. In playing the role of *reactor*, she is constantly suppressing her identity to the point where she may no longer even know who she is. The resentment over feeling "pushed around" will build steadily and constantly. Finally, she either explodes in rage or manifests countless psychological and somatic symptoms that reveal her frustration.

The gender fantasies we have all been raised on of establishing a "happily ever after" relationship between Miss Passive-Delicate-Fragile-Emotional   Female   and   Mr. Right-Successful-Rational-Dominant-Powerful-Strong Male are, from a look at their psychological underpinnings, an impossible dream. Still, it haunts most men and women and aborts their growth to the extent that they pursue it, certain that it can be found and made to work once they find the right partner.

For the man, the *actor-reactor* relationship lays the foundation for unending guilt and opens him up for the most hostile accusations. He can be blamed for everything, for, indeed, by being the *actor* he is responsible.

For other reasons, the *actor-reactor* interaction is lethal to the male. The *reactor* woman is out of touch with her aggression and consequently will not be prone to see her share of responsibility and negotiate in areas of conflict. She will tend only to blame, accuse, turn away in hurt or scream out in righteous rage. Meanwhile, he will be left to feel guilt-ridden and ugly. The statement "You have made me unhappy" rings primarily in the ears of the *actor*.

The aware, evolving woman understands that the rigidly controlling, dominating male is both destructive to her growth and a boring partner as well. Likewise, the self-caring, aware and growth-oriented man will realize how loaded, destructive and impossible is a relationship with a passive-submissive female *reactor* and will avoid and reject her for being lethal and destructive to his development as vigorously as a feminist would avoid the rigid *actor*, or, as he has so often been labeled, the "male chauvinist pig."

9. The "Macho Warrior" and His "Earth Mother" Wife

He never found her, though he looked
                Everywhere,
And he asked at her mother's house
        Was she there.

Sudden and swift and light as that
        The ties gave,
And he learned of finalities
        Besides the grave.

                Robert Frost, "The Hill Wife"

His underlying need is too strong, his anxieties and buried anger are too great. He cannot accurately see the woman he lives with.

He is the contemporary "macho warrior," self-contained, active, emotionally controlled, striving for dominance and out to stave off and slay the economic dragons. In the process he hustles, manipulates, smiles and claws his way to "material security" and the top of his sandpile.

In relationship to his "earth mother," he alternates erratically between sticky sentimentality and bursts of rage, withdrawn silence and hungry urgency, "set-me-free" demands and clinging dependency, and instant decisions and vacillating confusion. His manliness is in his erection, his ability to win, to provide, to be strong, unafraid, rational, certain and autonomous.

His "earth mother" wife is relatively faceless as she goes about the business of taking care of the house, buying and preparing food, waking everybody up and sending them off to bed, cleaning, shopping and reminding the family members of their responsibilities. Most of all, she reacts to the structure her "macho warrior" husband provides.

She has babies at a young age. A typical woman, she marries before she is twenty-two, while her husband is less than twenty-four. Within five years they have two children.

If he "lets her" or "wants her to," she takes a paying job besides her household functions. If he is a rigid, determined "macho warrior," however, he won't "let her" go to work. He'll say instead, "I want my wife at home to take care of the house and kids. Maybe that's not the way I'm supposed to think nowadays, but I know a woman can't divide up her time that way. Besides, I'm not going to come home after a hard day and help her scrub floors. I'm just not going to do it."

If economic necessity forces her to work, he feels ashamed and threatened. The shame is part of the guilt and self-hate that comes from "failing" as the *actor* who is responsible for the support but can't carry the load by himself. The threat is that she might become too independent and too worldly, and discover that she doesn't really need him, or that there is someone more interesting or "manly" available to her out in the "real world."

The "macho warrior"—"earth mother" relationship is a dream conceived in a fantasy heaven but lived out in a psychological hell. This interaction between him and her—she in her seemingly aggressionless, fragile, compassionate, self-denying, submissive, "nonsexual" role and he in his exaggerated aggressiveness, sexuality and intransigence in relationship to other men—can be seen in its purer form in some aspects of Latin-American culture.

The cult of Marianism, a movement within the Roman Catholic Church, has as its object the special veneration of the figure of the Virgin Mary. The "real woman," as she is pictured to be and as she behaves, is known for her infinite capacity for humility and sacrifice. No self-denial is too great, and there is no limit to her capacity for patience with the men in her life.[2] She is submissive to the demands of these men, be they husband, sons, father or brothers.[3] Beneath this overt submissiveness, however—a fact well known to the Latins—is an entirely different perception of them. Inwardly she believes that men are to be humored because they are *como niños* (like children) whose foolishness, stubbornness and lack of temperance must be forgiven because "they can't help the way they are."[4]

Furthermore, these "good women" do not enjoy coitus. They merely endure it when the duties of matrimony require it. When such a woman finds it necessary to even refer to sexual intercourse, as when speaking with a priest, a doctor or a trusted confidante, she describes it as "*Le hice el servicio*" ("I did him the service").[5]

Even her "macho" husband finds it necessary to reassure himself that she does not *really* enjoy sex. One Peruvian journalist illustrated the man's need to believe in the frigidity of "good" women by reporting typical male remarks such as, "So-and-so is a bad woman; once she even made love in the bathtub," or "American women (*gringas*) are all prostitutes. I know one who *even takes the initiative*."[6]

For the "macho," the lethal aspect of this inter-sex dance is vividly seen in the popular, widespread image of the black-clad, mantilla-draped woman, "kneeling before the altar, rosary in hand, while she prays for the souls of her sinful menfolk." It is seen even more directly in the classic religious figure of the *Mater dolorosa*, the teardrenched Mother who mourns for her lost Son.[7]

This Latin image is only an extreme variation of the American scenario, consisting of the impulsive, alcohol-prone man who runs around while his long-suffering, selfless "good woman" is waiting at home.

The "macho warrior" and his "earth mother" wife are alive and wearing many disguises in our culture. Family, friends and others are sentimentally moved when these beautiful young couples are embodied in the football player and his cheerleader girl friend, the military officer and his adoring French or Oriental wife; the construction worker or truck driver and his virginal, shy, wholesome, religious waitress or secretary bride; the energetic, "godlike" physician and his respectful, worshipful nurse-wife, who may even refer to him as "the doctor"; or the middle-management businessman, engineer or attorney who is ambitious, tough, dominant, rational, detached and unemotional and his demure, nurturing wife, waiting on him and supporting him in his struggles and battles with the world.

She has, at least temporarily, given up parts of her own identity for him, protecting his ego during lovemaking and rarely, if ever, confronting him or asserting herself directly on anything that would threaten his masculinity. She is "happy" to plan their social calendar, prepare the weekend gourmet meal for three other neighborhood couples, oversee the house, act as chauffeur for the children, run the errands and work at making herself attractive by regular appointments with the hairdresser, manicurist and dermatologist.

She is sufficiently amorphous in her way of being in the relationship for him to be able to perceive her passivity as mutuality and agreement, her accommodation to his rhythm as caring, her submissiveness as loyalty, her dependency as devotion, her lack of overt aggressiveness as fragility, vulnerability and helplessness and her sexual receptivity and accommodation as purity, adoring love and a sexual unworldliness.

In his perception of her sexually, he resembles the child who cannot really imagine his parents being lusting people who enjoy "doing it." For example, researchers queried Illinois State University students on their perceptions of their parents as sexual beings. One-fourth of those asked believed their parents no longer had sexual intercourse, and over 50 percent set the figure for sexual intercourse between their parents at once a month or less.[8]

Another part of the romantic, time-honored mythology about "his" woman that the traditional man clings to is that she is a mystery, ever changing and infinitely complex. Unable and in part unconsciously unwilling to see the psychological realities of the woman-person living with him, he chooses instead to see her as an unfathomable, emotionally unpredictable, Madonna-like "earth mother," driven to emotional extremes by raging hormones. In his mind, she is a devoted and fiercely protective mother, comfortably monogamous and satisfied to be in his shadow giving him background support in his worldly battles. He also sees her as somewhat of a saint with an endless capacity for understanding and forgiveness ("Sometimes I don't know how she's put up with me all these years; she's an angel") and self-denial ("She's content with so little"). What makes her even more spiritual and special in his eyes is that she has transcended the "grubby," animalistic drives and appetites that he feels rule and chain him. This makes him humbly grateful and even surprised that she would stay with him and still love him. In his eyes, this bewildering phenomenon is part of a cosmic master plan and mystery. And all of the qualities he sees in her—fragility, nonaggressiveness, childlike dependence and spiritual purity—validate his stance in the world as her protector and "macho warrior."

It has traditionally been part of his arrogance, and a tragic blind spot as well, that he has been unable to see and relate to her as she is rather than as he needs to believe she is, either separate or in relation to him. Of course, traditionally she has both consciously and unconsciously colluded with his need to avoid the total reality of her, as she suppressed significant parts of her identity in her relationship with him.

Traditionally, she did not express her needs for control or dominance overtly or directly. Her power came indirectly by withholding affection and sex, and through the guilt feelings he experienced when he saw her as someone who was easily hurt and damaged by him—a sensitive, fragile and helpless person. Because she reacted rather than acted and did not define herself clearly by asserting her needs and demands directly or by being openly aggressive, he could never be completely certain who she was, what she felt or really wanted and where she was going. Aggressive interaction of any kind was extinguished in her early conditioning. Therefore, hers became essentially a conflict-avoiding style. When issues of friction came up, her only possible response could be, "I don't want to argue (fight)." If he persisted, her tears would usually bring the encounter to an impasse.

This lack of overt assertiveness and aggression created the fantasy of a mystery. It reinforced his perception of her as spiritual and ethereal. Her non-confronting style and her vagueness allowed him to see in her what he wished. She was much like a Rorschach inkblot on which he could project his best or most negative fantasies. Occasionally she consciously reinforced this process. As one woman expressed it, "If he wanted 'nice,' I gave him 'nice.' When he wanted 'bitch,' I gave him 'bitch.' "

Her aggression has always been there, but because of its indirect, passive and hidden expression, he has not been able to recognize and deal with it. Professors Carroll, Smith, and Rosenberg, faculty members of the history and psychiatry departments of the University of Pennsylvania, studied the widespread phenomenon in nineteenth-century America of female hysteria and determined that hysteria was the result of cultural conditioning that socialized the woman into playing a weak, dependent role.

The hysteria would take the form of nausea, headaches, paralysis and so on. The most common form was the "fit," in which the woman writhed on the floor, tore her clothing, plucked out her hair and hit herself. These symptoms were attributed to "thin blood," masturbation or promiscuity, germs or sometimes simply the willfulness and evilness of the woman patient, who was seen as a vampire or pest. The underlying unconscious meaning of these symptoms was that through this "attack" she could vent her rage and dissatisfaction.[9]

Recent research comparing the psychological symptoms of the Anglo-American woman and her more passive-submissive Mexican-American counterpart as patients in psycho-therapy highlighted further these manifestations of repressed aggression. Mexican-American women were found to have four times as many somatic complaints, such as gastrointestinal disorders, and significantly higher frequencies of seventeen symptom categories ranging from crying spells to suicide attempts, withdrawal to the bedroom and staying in bed, eating difficulties, obesity, sleeplessness and temper tantrums.[10] Various researchers have observed considerable covert hostility on the part of the Mexican-American wives toward their husbands and have reported that since the hostility could not be expressed directly, it resulted in these symptom disturbances, which were sometimes as severe as catatonic symptomatology, psychologically interpreted as representing "frozen rage."

In contemporary American society the passive-submissive female frequently unconsciously becomes a "sickness tyrant" and then controls her husband and family with a wide and ever-changing repertoire of debilitating chronic symptoms. Or her repressed anger transforms into a bottomless well of complaints and she is seemingly incapable of being satisfied or happy.

When a woman transforms and begins to liberate herself, refusing to play any longer her self-denying "earth mother" role, allows her rage to emerge directly, reclaims her autonomous sexuality and refuses to remain in a dependent stance, her man often misinterprets these changes as being part of a psychiatric problem or a "nervous breakdown." He is convinced that she is "not herself," and encourages her to seek professional help in order to regain her "senses."

He has the picture in reverse. She *had been* "not herself" and is now "becoming herself." If indeed he is waiting for her to "come to her senses," he will be waiting for a long time. His rigid need to retain his unrealistic "macho" perception of her is backfiring. She is simply no longer being a figure on which he can project his rationalization of his own need to be the dominant, aggressive, sexual figure. He misinterprets her growth and sees it instead as emotional disturbance.

The "macho warrior" pays dearly for his inability to correctly perceive his woman or read the signals of the buildup of her dissatisfaction and resentment. Cook County Circuit Court Judge Margaret G. O'Malley commented on the behavior of some of these men who are suddenly abandoned by their transformed wives:

"I never used to believe it when a husband would come in after his wife filed and plead that he didn't want a divorce. I'd ask, 'Where have you been?' Now I realize they don't catch the signals until the point of no return."[11]

When this point of no return arrives and ends in divorce, "earth mother's" attitude changes considerably. She gets in touch with what has been buried or latent inside of herself during the marriage. What she says then must be paid attention to by any man not intent on impaling himself on his delusions of what "his" woman is really like.

Various researchers in Massachusetts interviewed recently separated or divorced women, who spoke with great honesty about their feelings.

"In separating from someone, you discover in yourself things that you had never felt before in your life," one woman said. "That's one of the things that really freaks you out. I've always used my mind to keep down anything I didn't like. And now I discover, wow, I can hate!"[12]

Another woman commented, "In many respects I really do hate my husband. But I don't want to think nothing but hate. You know, when I see him walking down the street, I don't want to think, 'I hope when you step off the corner you get run over.' "[13]

An attitude that would not fit the image of "earth mother" that many men have was expressed by one woman when she said, "My attitude toward men is—they are nice for friends, they're fine for sex. A good man is a guy who has his *own* money and enjoys sex. I don't want to take anything from anybody."[14]

Another ex—"earth mother" revealed, "There are times when I really miss my husband, and they're not flattering times—when a faucet leaks, a rat is in the garbage, taking a door off. They always know how to do it—I have to stare at it for an hour . . ."[15]

Other divorced women interviewed by researchers made similarly powerful remarks, such as:

1) "I don't know if I could accept responsibility of caring for a man. Men are big babies."[16]

2) "There are the horrors of loneliness—but the loneliness with him around was much more acute. I feel pride in making it on my own."[17]

3) "I'm more independent, more demanding than I used to be. I would have to trust a man a lot to give up my job again—this is my security."[18]

4) "It took so long to get myself back together. You can't put all your confidence, loyalties—eggs—in one basket."[19]

The "macho warrior" male, however, has yet to honestly acknowledge similar kinds of feelings. So he continues on in his blindly hopeful and urgent way trying to make the traditional "macho warrior"–"earth mother" relationship work.

A well-known professional athlete superstar saw an actress in a commercial on television and was very much taken by her. He arranged through friends of his in the television business to meet her. After a whirlwind courtship they were married, and the media gave this all-American dream couple extensive coverage.

One year later they were in the divorce courts, and his wife ungraciously informed a reporter that her soon-to-be ex-husband had brought a buddy along on their honeymoon and spent more time playing Ping-Pong with him than he did in his wife's company.

Clearly, she was impugning his masculinity in the eyes of the public, who probably believed there was something seriously wrong with him. After all, a "real man" would have been solely occupied with and jealously guarding his wife and would have had an ecstatic time spending hours in bed making love, interspersed only with sips of champagne and elegant meals, a few brief shopping sprees and moments in the sun or on the streets posturing for the envious world.

How many countless other "macho warrior" males have been hauntingly obsessed by feelings of inadequacy and self-doubt in similar situations because they did not experience with their women the kind of ecstasy and satisfaction they had expected on their honeymoon?

Because of their different psychological makeups, in the moment-to-moment process of being together the "macho warrior" man and his "earth mother" woman have precious little besides their fantasies of what ought to be to sustain an interesting, stimulating or pleasurable interaction. Many of these couples, in fact, could hardly make it through an afternoon alone together without feeling bored, yet they expect to maintain a lifetime of stimulating, enjoyable interaction.

The more gender polarized they are, in fact, in terms of his being "all man" and her being "all woman," the less of a psychological basis they have for relating to each other, because *they are opposite sides of a coin.* She is everything he is not, and vice versa. Consequently, they can only drive themselves into self-hating, hurtful and angry tailspins because they do not experience what they anticipated and were told by others they were going to. If indeed they remain together as a couple, the high-energy bursts of their initial romantic feelings will inevitably be transformed into deliberate, often painful efforts to be "nice" and "understanding" with each other. The relationship becomes a kind of stalemate, a painful, passionless compromise, as these couples try and force into existence what cannot exist authentically and naturally under their gender orientations and rigid role-playing interactions.

What is really often happening behind their closed doors was suggested in the following account written by a woman working in a model middle-class area of Los Angeles.

> For the past several years I have worked as a technician in a pharmacy in the San Fernando Valley. The neighborhood is middle-class and the customers are smiling, polite, clean-scrubbed professionals. Most of them visually fit the clean-cut American stereotype of USC graduates with season tickets to the Dodger games. In short, they are some of the "nicest" families in the Valley.
>
> When I first began working at the pharmacy, I was struck by the fact that although the volume of work was heavy (filling about 150 prescriptions a day), there were only half a dozen prescriptions a day for antibiotics, antihistamines, or oral contraceptives. The remainder were for mild tranquilizers, antidepressants, codeine with aspirin, sleeping pills, muscle relaxers, amphetamines, and codeine cough syrup. The amount of codeine cough syrup dispensed was staggering and the only real rival to Valium and Librium; however, the customer rarely appeared to have colds or to be ill in any way.
>
> I then began to notice that the heaviest work days were invariably Mondays, especially the Mondays after a long three or four day weekend. The refill business on Mondays often tripled our new business. Customers, both men and women, would begin calling as soon as we opened for Valium refills that they could pick up on their way to work; or with requests to call their doctor to ask for double the amount of their last prescription. When I mentioned this to the attending pharmacist, he laughed and said that the Monday "emergencies" were nothing compared to summer vacations.
>
> When vacations began in June, the Friday business picked up to the Monday level as families prepared to go camping, to Mexico, or to Europe for three weeks.

Husbands and wives with identical prescriptions got double amounts and joked about the necessity for having a "travel stash."

One Friday we ran out of Valium for two hours. One couple was so upset at not being able to get their prescriptions filled on the way to the airport (they were going to San Francisco for the weekend) that they decided to change their plane reservations to a late night flight, just in case the delivery man might be delayed in returning to the pharmacy with the new 10 milligram Valium supply.

I always ask unmarried or divorced people who deprecatingly label themselves as failures for their inability to achieve the romantic male-female ideal they obsessively strive for if they know any other couples intimately who do have the kind of relationship they so desperately seek for themselves. Invariably, they reply that it is difficult for them to think of even one. Clearly, these individuals who see themselves as "failures," along with many other frustrated couples who live in compromise relationships, are haunted by a fantasy which is constantly being reinforced by films, books, media, religion or the mythology they learned as children.

The sexual relationship is often the first to deteriorate into a non-satisfying experience for at least one of the partners, because its composition is that of a man focused on performance who is traumatized by a penis that is not instantly responsive and obedient, and a woman who approaches the sexual encounter with a relatively passive, receptive, reactive attitude, fearful and often unable to assert her needs and desires and often releasing her hidden anger by complaining about his insensitive touch or manner. "What do *you* want to do?" is her most typical answer to a question about her desires. Furthermore, the unexpressed resentment he must inevitably feel over the pressure to perform and her passivity, plus her resentment as she increasingly feels that she is being used mainly as a masturbatory receptacle, will also be reflected in their sexual experiences. Finally, his perception of her as special, different, fragile, even "sacred," and her perception of him as a man needing to be dominant, whose ego will be damaged by any honest feedback, will make both of them careful, fearful and inhibited about communicating honestly, to the point of rigid self-consciousness. This will further dam the sexual flow between them.

With growing problems in sex, the relationship, in order to survive, will probably change its focus from the bedroom to the kitchen and food preparation for the woman, and to the living room and munching and sipping beer in front of the television set for the man. On vacation, this will translate into endless rounds of dining at restaurants in search of ever more exotic foods, these excursions being interspersed with shopping sprees and time out for feeling ill after some of the meals.

At home, likewise, eating will become the primary, non-threatening vehicle for sharing. Its dynamic typically will be "she feeds" and "he eats." Her preparation of meals and having them on time, even when she is feeling harried and resents preparing them, will become symbolic of her "love" and involvement with him. In fact, when dinner is late, he may explode in rage because on a deeper level he unconsciously experiences this lateness as a rejection of himself.

Similarly, his enthusiastic eating of these meals will become symbolic of his communication with her and acceptance of her love. When he is particularly in need of proving something, he will eat seconds and thirds. Her willingness to continually get up and bring him food to nibble on without complaint will reassure him of her devotion.

People who wonder if they are caught in the deadening "macho warrior"—"earth mother" trap might use the following test. Imagine the relationship minus these eating rituals. Would it still be a pleasurable, playful, satisfying and interesting experience? The traditional relationship would probably not be able to stand this test.

In all other aspects of day-to-day living, "earth mother's" submissiveness, dependency, passivity, fragility and "purity"—the qualities he exalted when he first met her—will begin to grate, irritate and bore him. In fact, fatigue may set in whenever he's at home, as he feels himself drained by the constant need to be dominant and the lack of an energy-filled, honest and mutually responsi-